Professor D. Densil Morgan holds a pe  University, Wales, and is a member of the Inquiry based in Princeton in the United S of several books, including *The Humble C Christian Doctrine* (Canterbury Press, 2005 ..picted a volume on the reception of the theology of Karl Barth in Britain (T. & T. Clark, 2010).

The SPCK Introduction to ... series

The SPCK Introduction to

Karl Barth

D. Densil Morgan

First published in Great Britain in 2010

Society for Promoting Christian Knowledge
36 Causton Street
London SW1P 4ST
www.spckpublishing.co.uk

The author and publisher have made every effort to ensure that the external website
and email addresses included in this book are correct and up to date at the time
of going to press. The author and publisher are not responsible for the content,
quality or continuing accessibility of the sites.

Unless otherwise noted, Scripture quotations are taken from the New Revised Standard
Version of the Bible, Anglicized Edition, copyright © 1989, 1995 by the Division of
Christian Education of the National Council of the Churches of Christ in the United
States of America, and are used by permission. All rights reserved.

British Library Cataloguing-in-Publication Data
A catalogue record for this book is available from the British Library

ISBN 978–0–281–06045–0

1 3 5 7 9 10 8 6 4 2

Typeset by Graphicraft Ltd, Hong Kong
Printed in Great Britain by MPG

Produced on paper from sustainable forests

Contents

Preface

It is seldom wise for church historians to write books on systematic theology, but the opportunity to compose an introduction to the work of Karl Barth was one that I could hardly refuse. Two decades of undergraduate teaching on modern theology has sent me back repeatedly to the text of the *Church Dogmatics*, while my researches on twentieth-century church history have confirmed how influential Barth's doctrinal formulations have been. The welter of current publications on Barth augurs well for his impact on this century also. An earlier Welsh-language study of the *Church Dogmatics*, published in 1992, reflected both my own understanding of the subject and the state of scholarship at the time. Since then the study of Barth has expanded considerably, and there is now available a far richer body of work, from which a new consensus on Barth's abiding significance has emerged.

Sabbatical leave during the autumn of 2001 took me to Princeton Theological Seminary, where I had the opportunity of taking part in Professor George Hunsinger's reading group on *Church Dogmatics* IV, an experience that benefitted me enormously. In spring 2008, as a visiting scholar at Regent's Park College, Oxford, I embarked on a research project on the reception of Barth. The continuation of this project in the second half of 2008, as a member of the Center for Theological Inquiry at Princeton, afforded access to the neighbouring Theological Seminary's Barth Center, as well as time and stimulating company in which to reread and discuss Barth's work in depth. My gratitude to the principal and fellows of Regent's Park College, to the director, staff and colleagues at the Center for Theological Inquiry, is profound. I owe a debt to my friend and colleague,

Dr Robert Pope, for reading and commenting on the manu-
script, and for long discussions on Barth, theology and matters
pertaining to Church and academy generally. Rebecca Mulhearn
at SPCK has been an inspiration from the outset, while Neil
Whyte and Rima Devereaux have been painstaking in all aspects
of the copy-editing and desk editorial process.

Despite being sensitive to the need for gender-inclusive
language in referring to God, I have not attempted to excise
Barth's use of masculine pronouns. For one thing, this reflects
Barth's practice and that of his translators, influenced by the
prevailing culture of their generation. It also upholds the
conviction that the language of revelation, the Father being
known through the Son, is in some way normative. Orthodox
Christianity has always held to the fact that God is beyond
gender. The use of 'him' and 'himself', rather than the infelici-
tous 'Godself', should not be taken to mean that masculinity
pertains in any way to the nature or essence of God.

A large part of this short introduction to Karl Barth will
necessarily be concerned with the magnum opus that is *Church
Dogmatics*. While I have tried to make it possible to keep track,
in passing, of where the discussion is in relation to the complex
overarching structure of *Church Dogmatics*, the reader may
like first to become familiar with the tabular breakdown in
the Guide to further reading section towards the end of the
book.

As well as introducing the work of a giant of the past, I hope
that this short book will contribute to our understanding of
someone who has much to say to our present world and that
of the future.

Abbreviations

References to these, Barth's main original works (in their English versions), are given in place in the text. Other references are supplied in the Notes.

Bap.	*The Teaching of the Church Regarding Baptism*
CD I/1,	*Church Dogmatics*, followed by volume/part number
I/2 etc.	and page reference(s) if any (see A guide to further reading for a full breakdown with subtitles)
CL	*The Christian Life*
DC	*Deliverance to the Captives*
DE	*Die christliche Dogmatik im Entwurf*
DWG	*The Doctrine of the Word of God*
Ep. Rom.	*The Epistle to the Romans*
ET	*Evangelical Theology: An Introduction*
FGG	*Fragments Grave and Gay*
FT	*Final Testimonies*
GD	*The Göttingen Dogmatics: Instruction in the Christian Religion*
HG	*The Humanity of God*
HG&CL	*The Holy Ghost and the Christian Life*
HICMM	*How I Changed My Mind*
KGSG	*The Knowledge of God and the Service of God*
L	*Letters, 1961–68*
T&C	*Theology and Church: Shorter Writings 1920–28*
'Church'	'The concept of the Church'
'Herrmann'	'The principles of dogmatics according to Wilhelm Herrmann'
'Roman Catholicism'	'Roman Catholicism: a question to the Protestant Church'

'Schleiermacher and Ritschl'	'The Word in theology from Schleiermacher and Ritschl'
TET	*Theological Existence Today!*
TJC	*The Theology of John Calvin*
TS	*The Theology of Schleiermacher*
WGWM	*The Word of God and the Word of Man*
'Biblical questions'	'Biblical questions, insights and vistas'
'Christian's place'	'The Christian's place in society'
'Christian preaching'	'The need and promise of Christian preaching'
'Ethics'	'The problem of ethics today'
'Ministry'	'The Word of God and the task of ministry'
'New world'	'The strange new world within the Bible'
'Righteousness'	'The righteousness of God'

(§ denotes a 'paragraph' in *Church Dogmatics*, sometimes extending to scores or even hundreds of pages)

Date chart

1927	Publishes *Christian Dogmatics in Outline*

1927 Publishes *Christian Dogmatics in Outline*
1930 Appointed professor of systematics, Bonn
1931 Publishes volume on Anselm of Canterbury
1932 Publishes *Church Dogmatics (CD) I/1, Doctrine of the Word of God* (i)
1933 Hitler appointed German chancellor in January; demise of *Between the Times* due to theological tensions between Barth and Gogarten; publishes *Theological Existence Today!* in June
1934 Formation of German Confessing Church led by Martin Niemöller; Barmen Declaration, written principally by Barth, issued in May; prevented from teaching following refusal to swear loyalty oath to Hitler in November
1935 Expelled from Germany and appointed chair of systematics in home city of Basel in June
1937–8 Delivers Gifford Lectures in Aberdeen
1938 Publishes *CD I/2, Doctrine of the Word of God* (ii)
1939 Publishes *CD II/1, Doctrine of God* (i)
1942 Publishes *CD II/2, Doctrine of God* (ii)
1943 Lectures on 'The Church's teaching on baptism'
1945 Publishes *CD III/1, Doctrine of Creation* (i)
1948 Establishment of World Council of Churches in Amsterdam; publishes *CD III/2, Doctrine of Creation* (ii)
1950 Publishes *CD III/3, Doctrine of Creation* (iii)
1951 Publishes *CD III/4, Doctrine of Creation* (iv)
1953 Publishes *CD IV/1, Doctrine of Reconciliation* (i)
1955 Publishes *CD IV/2, Doctrine of Reconciliation* (ii)
1956 Lectures on 'The humanity of God'
1959 Publishes *CD IV/3 in two parts, Doctrine of Reconciliation* (iii)
1962 Retires; chair in systematics taken by Heinrich Ott; undertakes two-month journey to the USA; publishes *Evangelical Theology: An Introduction*
1966 Meets with Pope Paul VI in Rome to discuss doctrinal implications of the Second Vatican Council
1967 Publishes fragment of *CD IV/4, Doctrine of Baptism*
1968 Dies 10 December, aged 82

In what follows it may be useful to note that the German university year consists of two semesters: winter (mid-October to mid-February) and summer (mid-April to mid-July).

1

Young man Barth

The early years

Karl Barth was born in Basel, Switzerland, on 10 May 1886, the first son of Johann Friedrich ('Fritz') and Anna Barth. Fritz, like his father before him, was a minister of the Reformed Church and a scholar in his own right, having gained his doctorate in theology for a treatise on Tertullian, the early African church father. A conservative scholar, though not dogmatically so, he had undergone a conversion experience as a young man that had confirmed his loyalty to the Swiss Calvinism in which he had been raised. If Fritz was somewhat pensive and retiring, Anna was vivacious and outgoing. She too had been raised in a Reformed Church manse, though her background was more pietistically inclined than that of her husband. Her brother, father and grandfather were Reformed ministers in the city or environs of Basel, which was Fritz's home city as well. The couple had married in 1894 and two years later, a month before Karl was born, Fritz was called from his country parish to teach at the Basel College of Preachers, a seminary supplying biblically orthodox pastors for congregations of the Reformed Church.

Although his upbringing was strict, Karl would never find it oppressive. In fact both he and his brother Peter, who was born in 1898, would follow the family route into the pastorate. Peter, who died in 1940, became a Calvin scholar of repute.

The young family remained in Basel until 1889, when Fritz proceeded to Bern, some 60 miles to the south, to take up a

1

university post first as assistant lecturer in New Testament and patristics, and in 1895 the chair in early church history. There Karl and Peter were joined by a brother and two sisters: Heinrich, who would become a philosopher, Katharine, who died in childhood, and Gertrud.

Family life was boisterous and Karl, though engaged with his lessons, was hardly overtly studious. He was prepared for confirmation by Robert Aeschbacher, a dynamic young pastor and former pupil of Fritz's who shared his teacher's basic theological orientation and social concern. And like Fritz he was evangelical but always sensitive to orthodoxy's tendency to become ossified and lifeless. For him, sound theology had more to do with spiritual ebullience than strict notional correctness. Karl was so inspired that he felt he would have to know more. Following confirmation on 23 March 1902 he decided that he would become a theologian.

In theological terms, Bern at the time was something of a backwater. Despite this Karl, now 18, matriculated at the theological faculty of his father's university in October 1904 and spent the next four semesters, until summer 1906 (German university semesters numbering two a year), being instructed in the academic bases of Christian faith: Old and New Testaments, Hebrew and Greek, along with courses in church history and systematic theology. He was not inspired. He was surprised to find that his father was the most conservative member of the faculty. The speculative liberalism that dominated Bern theology was better typified by one rather ancient New Testament professor, a disciple of F. D. Baur's radical Tübingen school, who held that not one of St Paul's letters was authentic but all had been written as late as the second century. Most faculty members held to a superseded Hegelian idealism and rather deplored Albrecht Ritschl's insistence that Christianity was a historically based religion or it was nothing. If this old-fashioned idealism failed to resonate with Karl, his father's 'positivism' or middle-of-the-road orthodoxy fared little better. Fritz Barth's son was convinced that Protestant theology had more to offer, and in October 1906 he ventured abroad to study something more potent. Karl wanted to go to Marburg, where liberal theology was at its most vital and exciting, but Fritz, fearing his son would lose his doctrinal bearings, steered him to the more conservative Halle or Greifswald. They compromised, and decided that Karl should spend a single semester studying theology in Berlin.

The lure of liberalism

The ghost who stalked the corridors and classrooms of the University of Berlin was Friedrich Schleiermacher (1768–1834), its first professor of dogmatics, the so-called 'father of modern theology' and one whom Barth would always regard as 'this great, bold and truly religious theologian' (*T&C*, 'Schleiermacher' 159–99). It was Schleiermacher who had attempted most vigorously to bridge the divide between the naturalistic, non-revelatory preconceptions of the Enlightenment and the ongoing truths of the Protestant and evangelical faith. Although some of the Berlin professors were uncomfortable with the subjective romanticism of Schleiermacher's scheme and sensitive to the weaknesses of his use of the concept of 'feeling' as a key to understanding Christianity, others felt that his was the only valid way of doing theology in the modern world. Barth avoided the former – most pointedly his father's friend, the systematic theologian Reinhold Seeberg – and eagerly attended the lectures of the latter.

The one living scholar who made a deep impression on Barth in Berlin was the immensely erudite church historian Adolf von Harnack, who six years previously had charmed the university with a series of popular interfaculty lectures that would be translated as *What is Christianity?* For Harnack, there was a difference between the kernel of the faith and the transitory doctrinal husk in which it had been enveloped. The 'essence of Christianity', as the series had been titled, was simply the benign nature of God's fatherhood, the solidarity or 'brotherhood' of humankind and the infinite value of each individual soul. Such had been the essence of Jesus' teaching in the Gospels, which had been obscured by a speculative dogmatism beginning even in the New Testament with the complex theologies of St Paul and the apostle John. Whereas traditional Christianity had majored on the transcendent holiness of God, the sinfulness of humankind through the fall and the unique and supranatural quality of the atoning work of Christ, Harnack's God was immanent within creation, human life was imbued with inherent capabilities, and the concept of progress was taken for granted. This was hardly what Karl had been taught at home, and it diverged spectacularly from the sharp dichotomies of his inherited Reformed faith. Yet the young Swiss was transfixed.

If Barth was being drawn by the progressive teaching of Harnack, he was being even more stimulated by his own reading. It was at Berlin during the winter semester of 1906–7 that he first read and mastered Immanuel Kant's Enlightenment classic, *The Critique of Pure Reason* (1781), Schleiermacher's *Speeches on Religion to its Cultured Despisers* (1799) and the contemporary Marburg thinker Wilhelm Herrmann's *Ethics* (1901). It was Kant who, in a celebrated essay of 1796, had urged his contemporaries to cast away the props of external authority including, presumably, the Bible and the Church, and be bold enough to think for themselves. He had equally famously posited a divide between the phenomena of human knowledge and existence, and the *noumena* of ultimate reality – those things beyond reason's ability to grasp. These included God, freedom and immortality which, if they existed at all, could only be presupposed on the basis of intuition and people's ethical sense. Kant's God was a postulate of the moral consciousness. This deity was very much a God of the philosophers and not necessarily the Father of our Lord Jesus Christ.

A radical critique of traditional Christianity was implicit in the Enlightenment scheme. The deity of Christ, the New Testament miracles, the supposition that human nature was fundamentally impaired, were challenged and rejected. It had been left to Schleiermacher to devise a scheme that retained Christianity's religious potency while accepting much of the intellectual criticism inherent in the Enlightenment project. Having been brought up a Pietist, he retained an appreciation for the value of experiential religion and a warm faith in Jesus as saviour.

He was convinced, nevertheless, that the rationalists' critique could not be avoided. For Christians, at least Christ may still be the saviour, but it was no longer possible to think of him as the unique Son of God born of the Virgin, whose death was an atoning sacrifice for sin. He was, rather, the human bearer of God's gracious revelation to humankind. In his *Speeches*, Schleiermacher had argued that religion was not so much a set of doctrines or dogmas to be affirmed as a matter of experience, an emotional awareness of the divine. Whereas knowledge was confined to the phenomena of this world, as Kant had so compellingly shown, religion functioned in the realm of spiritual perceptions (or affections, the term used by psychologists of religion). What made a person religious was not, in the first instance, his or her innate ethical sense or the appropriation of a creed. It was, rather, the soul's awareness of the divine. The cultured despisers of late-eighteenth-century Berlin had rejected Christianity, believing it to be intellectually discredited. Schleiermacher, religion's equally cultured apologist, had insisted that it was not a matter of embracing implausible beliefs or practising a cold morality, but of being open to transcendent mystery that would enrich rather than impoverish lives. Christianity was the cultural form in which the universal religious impulse had expressed itself in the context of European life.

Schleiermacher's *Speeches* marked the beginning of an epoch in modern religious history and a new way of doing theology:

that of Protestant liberalism, which would be expressed most fully in the Berlin professor's systematic theology, *The Christian Faith* (1830). It was the early Schleiermacher of the *Speeches*, however, who would retain a hold on Barth's imagination, and for the next decade the theme of Karl's sermons would be the reality of the religious consciousness and God as a function of human experience of the divine. Schleiermacher, who had left his professorship at the University of Halle in 1807 to become pastor of Berlin's Trinity Church, a post he would combine with his teaching in the city's new university, would always retain a Christ-centred faith. In Barth's words:

> He was determined to preach Christ as the bearer of the great peace, as the original source and bringer of life. He pursued this purpose with an inner passion which is unmistakably clear to everyone, in his writings, in his sermons especially. And the method by which he sought to achieve it made a deep impression on his contemporaries.
>
> (*T&C*, 'Schleiermacher' 183)

It was not, however, an historical thinker but a contemporary figure who most affected Barth's awareness during the winter of 1906–7, namely, the Marburg theologian Wilhelm Herrmann (1846–1922). Herrmann's *Ethics* stirred him to the depths, but no sooner had he finished reading it than his single semester in Berlin ended, signalling his return to Bern.

His next rather dissolute semester at his home university was taken up not with theology but with unruly student affairs in which beer drinking and strong tobacco played a not insignificant part, while Karl clashed with his father over how religion should be expressed in the modern world. An increasingly despairing Fritz was insistent that his son should be exposed to sound theology rather than the heresies of liberal Marburg, and the next semester, autumn 1907, took Karl to conservative Tübingen, where the systematician Adolf Schlatter and a friend of his father's, the New Testament scholar Theodore Häring, reigned supreme.

It was, alas, a disaster: Karl rebelled forcefully not only against Fritz's positivism but against orthodoxy in all its forms.

Theology at Marburg

Sensing that he was in danger of alienating Karl terminally, Fritz relented, and in the spring of 1908 finally allowed his theologically wayward son to make the trek to Marburg. Karl would soon be revelling in the delights of a new world. On the one hand, he was afforded the opportunity of experiencing the teaching of such luminaries as Martin Rade, the engaging and open-hearted professor of social ethics, and sitting at the feet of the great Wilhelm Herrmann himself, and on the other, of striking up friendships with other students of his own ilk. One of them, his fellow Swiss Eduard Thurneysen (1888–1977), who happened to be the son of one of Fritz Barth's oldest friends, would in turn become Karl's closest associate in the momentous break with liberalism that would occur a decade or so later. But Herrmann was the star. 'Herrmann', Barth would reminisce in 1925, 'was *the* theological teacher of my student days. The day twenty years ago in Berlin when I first read his *Ethik* I remember as if it were today ... I can say that on that day I believe my own deep interest in theology began' (*T&C*, 'Herrmann' 238–71 [238]).

Herrmann belonged to the school of liberal theologians who had taken their lead from Albrecht Ritschl (1822–89). Unlike Schleiermacher, Ritschl was uncomfortable with the concept of feeling, emotion and subjective experience as the criteria for discovering theological truth, but was convinced that Christianity was, in essence, a phenomenon of history. History was open to scholarly scrutiny, and it was along historical lines that God's disclosure of himself could be ascertained. Ritschl was an avowed enemy of metaphysics and abhorred Hegel's idealism as a corruption of religious truth. Rather than existing as some abstract 'Absolute' only tangentially connected to ordinary existence, God had committed himself to the historical process and could be known through the moral and spiritual impact he had made on humankind. This had occurred exquisitely in the person of Jesus Christ.

Unlike the radical New Testament critics of the Tübingen school, Ritschl believed that the Gospels were dependable portraits of actual events showing that the person of Jesus had made a profound impact on the lives of his followers. While he rejected the way complex and unnecessary doctrines had later evolved, obscuring the immediacy of the historical Christ, there was no doubt that Jesus was the bearer of a divine salvation and that God had been uniquely active in his life. Although not directly perceptible by human means, God was unquestionably discernible through the moral effect he had on human life. For those not prejudiced against God, God's existence could be perceived in the actions of those who believed in him. History revealed that Jesus had preached the coming of God's kingdom, that the lives of those who had responded to his proclamation had been changed and that human society had improved as a result. This reality was still open for people within the Church, and for subsequent believers Jesus, who could be accessed by means of the New Testament Gospels, conveyed the value of God to us.

By the time Barth arrived in Marburg, Ritschl's scheme had long been assailed by theologians on the left and on the right. Conservatives believed that he had conceded too much to Kant in asserting that God was not directly perceptible to human consciousness, and accused him of undermining the factual nature of such key doctrines as Christ's objective divinity and the miraculous occurrences that, in the New Testament, had accompanied the proclamation of God's kingdom. Radicals and progressives, however, were convinced that his historicism had not gone far enough. If revelation occurred within the realm of sober, objective, mundane history, then surely it could not be confined to the sphere of the Christian Church. Was it not special pleading to claim that God was only to be found in Jesus and the impact he had made on his followers?

It was Ernst Troeltsch, one of Ritschl's most brilliant pupils, who had asserted this view most cogently. Historical research was bound by the historical method and not dogmatic convictions concerning the religious value of Christ. As an historical phenomenon, Christianity could claim no special dispensation. It was, in fact, only one religion among many, and all the scholar could do was study the thought, worship and religious activity of humankind. Scholarly objectivity demanded, therefore, that theology should yield its privileged status and become a species of anthropology. This was the only thing plausible within the human realm. By the 1890s, Troeltsch's 'History of Religions School' had established itself firmly on the radical edge of the theological endeavour.

Wilhelm Herrmann, who had been appointed to Marburg's primary theological chair in 1879, was acutely aware of Troeltsch's critique. Like Ritschl, he rejected the dominance of metaphysics within the theological realm and lamented the way in which the discipline had allowed itself so often to be ruled by alien philosophies and non-theological modes of thought. He also believed that God had revealed himself in the historical Christ, and that Jesus of Nazareth was amenable to objective research. However, on balance, what was most important was the independent validity of Christianity and its self-authenticating nature as a faith. Like his mentors, Herrmann was also a man of the Church. He was unwilling to allow the unique nature of Christianity to be dissipated through some generalized process of human religiosity. Yet Troeltsch had a point. The problem was how best to utilize ordinary historical criteria and preserve the revelatory uniqueness that the Christian faith had always claimed for itself. The answer, for Herrmann, was in the inner life of Jesus, the Christ.

Christ existed in history, as a man among men. Christ purported to be God's revelation to humankind, and the impact he had had certainly gave credence to his claim. Divine revelation, however, was not outwardly perceptible to the observer and as such was not immediately or directly accessible to historical research. The outer phenomena of Christ's life, his actions and teaching, occurred within the mundane, observable, historical realm, but his inner experience, namely, his unsullied communion with his heavenly Father, was obscured from the world. It was this quality of relationship that, in fact, constituted Christ's essential divinity. It was also the link, according to Herrmann, between revelation and history, and the unique juncture at which true religion occurred. The theologian's most popular work, *The Communion of the Christian with God* (1886), showed how the individual believer, in emulating Christ, could experience this reality, though in a very attenuated and inadequate way. Christ, though, was sinless, the depth of his devotion perfect, whereas human religion, even at its best, was but a pale shadow of that which had become incarnate in Christ. Whereas Ritschl placed his emphasis on the Jesus of history and his proclamation of the kingdom, Herrmann wrote much on the inner life of believers and their Lord. Echoing Schleiermacher, he held that religion, though existing within the flow of objective history, was in essence a matter of experiencing transcendent reality within the soul.

Barth spent three splendid semesters in Marburg, first from April to September 1908, and following graduation with second-class honours, until September 1909. He attended Herrmann's lectures on the introduction to dogmatics as well as his course on ethics, and although he would have decisively to reject the psychologizing aspects of his theology in favour of a definite trinitarianism rooted in God's active self-revelation in his Word, he would always hold his teacher in high esteem. 'For twelve years I was a minister, as all of you are,' he told a meeting of clergy in 1922. 'I *had* my theology. It was not really mine, to be sure, but that of my unforgotten teacher, Wilhelm Herrmann, grafted upon the principles [of the Reformed Church] which

I had learned ... in my native home' (*WGWM*, 'Christian preaching' 67–135 [100]). Despite his overwhelming liberalism, Herrmann had held to the self-authenticating nature of faith, the objective reality of God, knowledge of whom could only be obtained by God's own gracious revelation of himself, and the participatory aspect of religious truth: Christian truth was not speculative but only yielded itself to those who actively submitted to its claims: 'It was *he*', wrote Barth, 'who showed me that truth' (*T&C*, 'Herrmann' 239). Even after the sea change that occurred in Barth's thinking following the tumultuous years of the First World War, elements of continuity would remain:

> I cannot deny that through the years I have become a somewhat surprising disciple of Herrmann ... but I could never inwardly agree that I had really turned away from my teacher. Nor can I so agree today.
>
> (*T&C*, 'Herrmann' 238–9)

Ordination

Karl Barth was ordained into the ministry of the Swiss Reformed Church on 4 November 1908, in the cathedral at Bern. He was by now 22 years old. The ordination rite was administered by his father, who also delivered the charge. Rather than taking up pastoral responsibilities immediately, Karl returned to Marburg, where he had been appointed assistant to Martin Rade, who combined his professorial responsibilities in social ethics with the editorship of the leading journal of the Protestant liberals, *The Christian World*. Barth's next 11 months would afford him ample time to take his studies further, and he even published a handful of scholarly articles in the liberal mould. Yet the pastoral ministry beckoned, and on 26 September 1909 he was inducted as assistant pastor of the Reformed Church in Geneva, with special responsibility for the German-speaking congregation. Barth's senior pastor was a fellow German Swiss, Adolf Keller, a remarkable figure who would gain prominence in the 1920s as an ecumenical statesman and who would be a key figure in the early reception of Barth's theology in Britain and the United States. The young minister threw himself into the pastoral round, spending time in sermon preparation, confirmation classes, sick visiting and poor relief. Attendance at Sunday services was sparse, and Barth experienced at first hand the way in which the menfolk especially were alienated from the Church, despite its being nominally Reformed. His experience-based liberalism, however, remained intact, and he exhorted his flock to emulate Jesus in hastening the kingdom by subjecting themselves fully to the Father's will. Jesus, he claimed, was not so much God as 'our way to the Father'; yet we can still know him 'by an experience'. Through our devotion and obedience, 'the same thing that happened in Jesus happens in us'. 'The power and life that you sense in him can become your power and life.'[1] It was an incongruous message, preached Sunday by Sunday from John Calvin's actual pulpit in the auditorium where the great Reformer had taught next to the cathedral of St Pierre.

Barth's 18 months in Geneva were highly rewarding. He was diligent, cheerful and wholly content. In May 1911 he became engaged to Nelly Hoffmann, the daughter of a St Gallen lawyer who had died when Nelly was only a year old. Nelly had thereafter been brought up by her mother in Geneva. She had been a faithful member of Karl's first confirmation class and was a talented musician. They would be married two years later when she had reached the age of 20 and Karl was 27. By then he had left his Geneva assistantship to become the sole pastor of the Reformed Church parish of Safenwil in the canton of Aargau, some 40 miles from Basel, where of course he had been born.

2

The pastor of Safenwil

'Comrade Pastor'

The semi-agrarian community of Safenwil, halfway between Basel and Zürich, had a population of 1,500 of whom 600 worked in the local textile factories and woollen mills. It was overwhelmingly Protestant, and the owner of one of the factories and his family were prominent in the local Reformed congregation. No sooner had he arrived, in July 1911, than the newly instituted pastor found himself taking sides in the rift already prevalent between the industrialists and their workers. Barth had been struck by the social question during his assistantship in Geneva, but was now faced with the predicament within his own church fellowship. 'In the class conflict which I saw concretely before me in my congregation,' he wrote,

> I was touched for the first time by the real problems of real life. The result was that for some years ... my only theological work consisted of the careful preparation of sermons and classes. What I really studied were factory acts, safety laws and trades unionism, and my attention was claimed by violent local and cantonal struggles on behalf of the workers.[1]

In a way this was quite unexpected. Although Karl's father Fritz was possessed of a social conscience, since being called to the professorate (see Chapter 1) he had poured all his energies into his academic work and provided his family with a typically bourgeois if pious upbringing. The theology Karl had imbibed in Berlin, Tübingen and Marburg, where 'I absorbed Herrmann through every pore',[2] was even less politically engaged. All his teachers had been conservatively inclined German conformists with a distaste for anything approaching social radicalism. For them, the Swiss democratic system was wholly alien and potentially subversive. Switzerland, however, was not Germany, and unlike Lutheranism, with its ingrained deference to authority, the Reformed tradition possessed a dissident ethos that could, in certain circumstances, become markedly radical. Barth's training in liberal individualism hardly provided the apparatus to understand systemic unrighteousness or structural evil, but soon he was immersing himself in the works of socialist theorists and showing a doughty solidarity with Safenwil's proletariat. Before long he was being addressed as 'Comrade Pastor'. The more staid elements within his congregation hardly knew how to respond.

The Religious Socialist movement that had been established in 1906 had swept through the Swiss Reformed Churches, attracting many of the more idealistic young ministers, especially during Barth's semesters abroad. Standing in the background was the charismatic preacher Christoph Blumhart, from Bad Boll in Germany, who had blended eschatological revivalism with radical politics. But the movement's leading theoretician in Switzerland was the Zürich pastor Hermann Kutter. Kutter's liberationist theology was heavily influenced by Marxist teaching, and its principal practitioner was Leonhard Ragaz, minister of Basel Cathedral and the movement's founding chairman. Both taught that the socialist movement was a reproach to the Churches' timid conformity, and believed that God was at work advancing his kingdom, despite the atheism and materialism many of the workers espoused. Inspired especially by Kutter's ideas, Barth urged Safenwil's ill-paid artisans to unionize, and lectured on the compatibility of Christianity with the socialist cause. Unlike Kutter he never became a Marxist, but in good liberal fashion sought the enlightenment of individuals whose moral renewal would lead to a revolution in social attitudes. Whereas Marx believed there to be immutable economic laws within the historical process, Barth was still an ethical idealist. He would, however, find himself preaching God's kingdom not as an internalized principle, as Adolf von Harnack had taught, but as a historical reality with concrete social implications.

Disenchantment

Notwithstanding his energetic championing of workers' rights, Barth remained foremost a devoted parish minister. Sadness prevailed in February 1912 when Fritz Barth died at the relatively early age of 55. Despite the earlier tensions between them, Karl retained a respect for his father's scholarship and admiration for his piety, and before long he would find himself in substantial agreement with the orthodoxy that as a student he felt destined to reject. Nevertheless, sorrow was eclipsed by joy when Nelly Hoffmann arrived in Safenwil to share the life of the manse. They were married in March 1913 and a year later Franziska, their first child, was born. She would be joined by Marcus in 1915 and Christoph in 1917, both of whom would become Reformed ministers and theologians in their own right. Another key event was the arrival in June 1914 of Eduard Thurneysen, an associate from Marburg days, as pastor of the neighbouring village of Leutwil. An almost daily correspondence would complement their weekly meetings, in which they would become progressively disenchanted with their acquired liberalism and begin hammering out a new theology centring on the Word of God. 'Once in the ministry I found myself . . . being forced back at every point to the specific *minister's* problem, the *sermon*' (*WGWM*, 'Christian preaching' 67–135 [100]). A theology of experience seemed not to be able to speak to the pastoral needs of a village congregation, while the intractable problems of industrial unrest demanded more than an idealistic social gospel for their solution. Thurneysen and Barth agonized over the preacher's dilemma. 'Before him lies the Bible, full of mystery; and before him are seated his more or less numerous hearers, also full of mystery . . . *What now?* asks the minister' (*WGWM*, 'Christian preaching' 104). It was this element of expectation and mystery that had been lost in liberalism's all too comfortable equating of human progress with the transcendent Word of God. From late 1914 onwards, both Barth and Thurneysen would be drawn to the text and narrative of the Bible in a radically new way.

Through the ten years of his Safenwil pastorate Barth took his ministerial responsibilities seriously. He prepared his sermons meticulously and took especial care with confirmation classes. 'Karl Barth did not have an easy time with his congregation,' reported Thurneysen, 'nor did his congregation have an easy time with him.'[3] By the end of 1913 he had lost most of his church officers, some of whom were related to the textile manufacturer whose practices he had opposed, but he soon gained a new set of officials who took less umbrage at his political activities. As in Geneva, congregations were never large and often unresponsive, but despite his socialist views his sermons were not in any way partisan. It was clear, however, that he was moving away from the immanentism of his liberal stance and emphasizing such truths as the holiness of God and the divine wrath against human unrighteousness (not least that unmasked by capitalist greed) that questioned the bland optimism of the dogma of inevitable progress. Following a series of sermons on the prophet Amos he also developed a searing critique of 'religion' as such. In fact Barth was having to review his whole concept of God. 'What do sceptics know about life and death questions?' he wrote to his brother Peter years later:

> They leave the question 'does God exist?' open. Surely the sceptic's question always leaves one essentially as one was before, unshaken. Doesn't this become dangerous only *if*

and *because* God is? ... That is the question I failed to recognize as a student or as a young pastor. It is the question which came down on me like a ton of bricks round about 1915.[4]

God's existence was not a matter merely of interest or of speculation, neither was God's presence a comforting affirmation of the status quo.

And then, like a thunder clap, came the First World War. 'One day in early August 1914 stands out in my personal memory as a black day,' wrote Barth in a paragraph that has been quoted repeatedly:

> Ninety-three German intellectuals impressed public opinion by their proclamation in support of the war policy of Wilhelm II and his counsellors. Among these intellectuals I discovered to my horror almost all of my theological teachers whom I had greatly venerated. In despair over what this indicated about the signs of the time I suddenly realized that I could not any longer follow either their ethics and dogmatics or understanding of the Bible or of history. For me at least, nineteenth-century theology no longer held any future.   (*HG* 12–13)

For Barth, this 'horrible manifesto' was 'almost even worse than the violation of Belgian neutrality' (*TS* 263). It was as though the unconditional truths of the gospel had been suspended and an imperial war theology put in their place. What was worse was that Harnack, Herrmann and the rest had supported this unreservedly. 'It is truly sad!' wrote Barth to Thurneysen on 4 September. 'Marburg and German civilization have lost something in my eyes by this breakdown, and indeed forever.'[5] Already disillusioned by the swelling weaknesses of liberalism, Barth and Thurneysen knew they had to find an alternative theology in which God's reality would assert itself once more.

Back to the Bible

After having mused about how best to respond to the spiritual challenge that was facing them, Barth and his colleague decided that they needed to return to 'the strange new world within the Bible'. For Barth, this would mean a serious study of St Paul's Epistle to the Romans, which began in earnest in June 1916. For the two young ministers of the Reformed Church, the Bible was utterly familiar and the least strange book in the world. But that, of course, was the point. Critical theology had taken the Bible for granted, explaining it as a human construct, a compendium of experiences, a religious textbook in which the disconcerting presence of God had been domesticated and lost. But were the Bible to be read not from the perspective of subjective religiosity but from one in which God's unique and gracious sovereignty was presupposed, the result would be unexpectedly different. 'When *God* enters, history for the while ceases to be', claimed Barth in a key address of September 1916, '. . . for something wholly different and new begins, a history with its own distinct grounds, possibilities and hypotheses . . . a new world projects itself into our old ordinary world . . . [namely] the world of *God*' (*WGWM*, 'New world' 28–50 [37]).

Yet even such a standpoint as this was not devoid of ambiguities. Barth was acutely conscious that all thought and talk of God presupposed the active participation of those doing the thinking and talking. This was just as true of conservative orthodoxy as of the liberalism that had dominated Protestant theology from the days of Kant onward. What now struck Barth with enormous force was that the God to whom the Bible witnessed was complete in himself, wholly independent of human appropriation, only accessible through himself by allowing himself to be known. In other words, in order for God to be known at all, a process of *self-revelation* would have to occur. Barth had already reacted violently against the 'God' of idealism who, despite being decked out in Christian colours, was merely a projection of the human spirit:

> This god is really an unrighteous god and it is high time for us to declare ourselves thoroughgoing doubters, sceptics, scoffers and atheists in regard to him ... this god, to whom we have built the tower of Babel, is not God. He is an idol. He is dead.
>
> (*WGWM*, 'The righteousness of God' 9–27 [22])

What the Bible revealed was not an immanent *or* transcendent reality that could be accessed by human knowledge, but a God who deigned to make himself known: 'It is not the right human thoughts about God which form the content of the Bible, but the right divine thoughts about men' (*WGWM*, 'New world' 43).

For Karl Barth, the transformation came in the process of writing his commentary on the Epistle to the Romans, in which he had been absorbed since the summer of 1916. What had struck him throughout the process of composition had been the utter strangeness of the biblical material:

> During the work it was often as though I were being looked at by something from afar, from Asia Minor or Corinth, something very ancient, early oriental, indefinably sunny, wild, original, that somehow is hidden behind these sentences and is so ready to let itself be drawn forth by every new generation. *Paul* – what a man he must have been, and what people also for whom he could so sketch and hint at these pithy things in a few muddled fragments! I shudder often in such company ... And then *behind Paul*: what realities those must have been that could set this man in motion in such a way.[6]

The volume was submitted to the publishers in August 1918, appeared in December and instantly made a deep impression. Devoid of the technicalities of critical scholarship, it expounded the text of the epistle with an immediacy that was startling: 'The reader will detect for himself that it has been written with a joyful sense of discovery. The mighty voice of Paul was new to me, and if to me no doubt to many others also' (*Ep. Rom.* 2). Gone were the suppositions of Protestant liberalism: that God was immanent within the world; that knowledge of God was innate in the human soul; that mundane history was the plane on which God operated and was therefore accessible to disinterested scholarly investigation; and that humanity could be synthesized with the divine. According to this new Biblicism, God was God, categorically different from humankind, and the gospel was God's gracious turning to humankind through the active obedience of Christ, the divine Son.

Although *The Epistle to the Romans* was aimed at the scholarly community and theologically informed pastors such as Barth himself, Barth's main preoccupation was with his flock. The international crises that followed the Russian revolution of 1917 and Germany's defeat a year later impacted on Switzerland as well, and by 1919 there were profound divisions throughout the canton of Aargau. As a member of the Social Democratic Party, the pastor was still heavily involved in political activities, while his support for the general strike the summer before had been deeply divisive. The Russian revolution had struck fear into many, and although Barth had no truck with either Marxism or violent revolution, his active support for the workers made him intensely unpopular among Safenwil's bourgeoisie. Ironically, this commitment to concrete social change went hand in hand with his alienation from Religious Socialism. He was by now openly critical of Hermann Kutter's Marxist-tinged liberation theology and Leonhard Ragaz's activist pragmatism. Barth now reasoned that the kingdom to which the New Testament testified was an eschatological reality for which Christ's resurrection from the dead was the key. God's kingdom did not grow out of the possibilities lying ready to hand on the surface of history, rather it broke into history from beyond as God saw fit according to his sovereign rule. Political agitation for a more just society could only be a parable of the kingdom and not a humanly wrought aspect of the kingdom's coming. What was more, political activity possessed its own integrity in which Christians should be engaged for its own sake. Ethical obedience was a correlate of, rather than a participation in, the advent of God's kingdom within the world.

The Tambach lecture

An opportunity came to expound these thoughts in a conference of Religious Socialists and others at Tambach in the German state of Thuringia in September 1919. The lecture would be pivotal in Barth's career, and it introduced him to a vastly wider sphere of influence. Affected by the uncertainty that followed Germany's wartime defeat, a younger generation was seeking guidance and inspiration. Barth, who had been invited as a replacement speaker for the more celebrated Ragaz, talked on the unremarkable theme of 'the Christian's place in society'. His address, however, was anything but unremarkable. It was, in fact, highly technical and in parts obscure, but delivered with such verve and startling evocation as to make an immediate impression on all.

The Christian, Barth stated, was no less than Christ himself, obliquely active in the world but on his terms and in his unique way. There was no intrinsic link between Christ and society or between human striving and the righteousness of God. God retained his absolute sovereignty, yet men and women were bidden to obedience despite the divide: 'There *is* no continuity leading from analogy over into divine reality' (*WGWM*, 'Christian's place' 272–327). God, he claimed, was the 'Wholly Other' – an appropriate phrase to describe God that Thurneysen had laconically suggested a few years before – yet remained the Creator and redeemer of humankind, who calls men and women not to co-operate with him but to be obedient to their relative tasks. However concrete, historical and realistic the biblical kingdom was, it nevertheless breaks in from beyond. Its reality was eschatological and its relation to mundane history indirect: 'The *resurrection* of Jesus Christ from the dead is the power which moves both the world and us, *because* it is the appearance in our corporeality of a *totaliter aliter* ("wholly other") constituted corporeality' (*WGWM*, 'Christian's place' 323). This was not a spiritualized, ahistorical resurrection or something less than physical or corporeal, but it was the only sort of physicality appropriate to the reality of God. Barth later wrote:

> That I had thought and expressed things for which I would have to answer before a wider public first began to be clear to me when, in September 1919, I was invited to give an address at the Religious Social Conference at Tambach, and for the first time saw the completely altered situation in post-war Germany.[7]

Much of the content of his lecture had been implied in the Romans commentary, but now he found a new audience who had no use for the older liberalism and were openly receptive to his specific insights. 'Here I suddenly found a circle, and the prospect of further circles, of people to whose unrest my efforts promised answers which at once became new questions in the fresh contacts with these German contemporaries.'[8] The upshot was that the Romans volume found a whole sector of new readers who were passionate to make its theology their own.

Almost immediately after his reputation had been established in Germany, Barth felt that the commentary needed to be revised. His biblical studies had taken him further into the Pauline corpus, into Ephesians and Corinthians especially, but had also led him into dialogue with the nineteenth-century Danish existentialist, Søren Kierkegaard, and the later radical Basel New Testament scholar, Franz Overbeck, who had in fact been an atheist and critic of modern Christianity. And Barth's brother, Heinrich, now a professional philosopher, had given him fresh insights into the work of Kant. Thurneysen had also encouraged him to read the novels of Fyodor Dostoevsky, for their profound treatment of matters of faith. Barth was also uncomfortable with the concept of God's kingdom as expounded previously, which he now felt was insufficiently orientated towards God's future. Conversations at a student conference in April 1920 convinced Barth more than ever that the old liberalism little realized the extent to which it was being challenged 'in a time when we know the difference between false and true Christianity as we do today – when the failure of the relative type, consisting of experience, metaphysics and history, is so palpably, so unmistakably before our eyes' (*WGWM*, 'Biblical questions' 51–96). His old teacher Adolf von Harnack, who was also present as a speaker, was saddened and perplexed. For Harnack, Barth's positive reassessment of the doctrine of election, his diastasis between humankind and God, the key significance he gave to the concept of resurrection and the mystery of the forgiveness of sins – 'To me this fact of "forgiveness" is even more astonishing than the raising of Lazarus' – was incomprehensible (*WGWM*, 'Biblical questions' 92). The older generation hardly understood the vehemence with which its presuppositions were being assailed.

The second Romans commentary

Barth began rewriting Romans in October 1920. The second edition would be considerably bulkier than the first and contain sharper antitheses, an extravagant use of dialectical terminology and more striking metaphors, many of which were taken from the battlefield and, curiously, from the world of mathematics. The coming of Christ was 'the crater made at the percussion point of an exploding shell'; the gospel was 'a crater formed by [an] explosion'; in Christ 'two planes intersect . . . the unknown world cuts the known world', while in the resurrection the Holy Spirit touches the present age 'as a tangent touches a circle, that is, without touching it' (*Ep. Rom.* 29, 36, 29, 30). The eschatological orientation was made even more emphatic: 'If Christianity be not altogether thoroughgoing eschatology, there remains in it no relationship whatever with Christ' (*Ep. Rom.* 314). The theme running through the whole was God's disconcerting and disorientating deity, which implied an undermining of humankind's moral, ethical and religious quest per se. The commentary included a ferocious polemic against 'religion', which Barth, an ordained clergyman, regarded as a purely human endeavour independent of God, preventing people from knowing the real God and responding to his radical claim on their lives. The true God was remote, alien and hidden, unveiling himself indirectly through the crisis of the gospel. There was no continuity or affinity between the human and the divine, rather disruption, confrontation and judgement. Even humility and repentance, where they represented some sort of claim on God, were anathema.

What Barth was *not* doing, though it was not always clear at the time, was changing the emphasis from divine immanence to transcendence. That would have been a commonplace that would have left the conventional theology intact. Rather he was challenging wholesale the notion of God's accessibility through human perception, whether liberal or orthodox. God, he claimed vehemently, was beyond the bounds of independent human thought: 'God . . . is distinguished qualitatively from men and from everything human and must never be identified with anything we must name, or experience, or conceive, or worship' (*Ep. Rom.* 330). God was *God*, breaking forth on his terms, as a flash of lightning, a tangent glancing a circle, oblique and hidden even in the action of self-revelation, and appropriated in the crisis of faith. God was, in fact, 'pure negation' (*Ep. Rom.* 141).

In his passion to establish God's absolute deity, Barth left more than a few hostages to fortune. Christ, he claimed, *revealed* himself to be *hidden,* a paradox that caused critics to accuse him of being either perverse or religiously a sceptic, while the concept of Christ's resurrection occurring on a plane not amenable to historical proof gave rise to the idea that he rejected its corporeal aspect totally: 'The resurrection is not an event in history at all' (*Ep. Rom.* 30). Barth was not, in fact, disputing either an actual and concrete revelation in history or the need for human appropriation of that revelation in faith, but he was clearing the ground for the sort of response that was in keeping with the proper nature of the divine. His protest was against any independent means of appropriating God's revelation that took for granted human beings' *natural* ability to respond. This had been the mistake of mainstream Protestant theology for a century and a half.

> The grace, which the theologians of the time [between Schleiermacher and Ritschl] described so beautifully as free, did not remain free for them. They claimed it as a right, a certainty, a possession of the Christian, the so-called believing Christian.
> (*T&C,* 'Schleiermacher and Ritschl' 200–16 [216])

God's grace was anything but a certainty and a possession and a right. It could not be accessed straightforwardly but only dialectically: 'It is not against faith that we are warned,' he claimed, 'but against OUR faith' (*Ep. Rom.* 514). True faith centred on Christ, the resurrected Lord, who came to humankind miraculously from beyond. Barth was yet to work out an adequate Incarnation theology – the concept of a line *touching* a circle was patently insufficient – or a valid atonement doctrine: these tasks could hardly be avoided now that he had taken Paul as his lead. On the whole, however, his meaning was clear. There was no doubt that the volume was a tour de force. As Karl Adam, the Catholic theologian, was memorably to state: 'The commentary on the Romans fell like a bomb on the playground of the theologians.'[9]

The second edition of *The Epistle to the Romans* was completed in a remarkable 11 months, a Herculean task considering Barth's ongoing parish work, the pressures he was now under to contribute to the wider theological world, and his family responsibilities: Matthias, Nelly's and Karl's fourth child, was born in April 1921. 'This hot summer will ever be unforgettable to me,' he informed Thurneysen a month later. 'I amble like a drunk man back and forth between writing desk, dining table and bed, travelling each kilometre with my eye already on the next one.'[10] What increased the pressure extraordinarily was the fact that he had been sounded out early in the year for a newly created post of honorary professor of Reformed theology in the Lower Saxon university town of Göttingen. The Göttingen faculty was Lutheran and Barth, were he to accept the position, would be the sole representative of Calvinistic theology. He would also be very junior and, not possessing a doctoral degree, potentially very exposed. What was more, apart from being taught to revere the Reformed tradition in which he had been raised, he knew very little about Calvin's theology as such. There was no doubt, however, that the sponsors of the chair, namely, the Reformed Church of Saxony, with the financial support of the American Presbyterians, were insistent that the pastor of the obscure Swiss parish of Safenwil was *the* person to represent the tradition of John Calvin in that bastion of Lutheranism. The official invitation came in May, and on 13 October, having spent ten rich and unforgettable years among the people of his alpine charge in Aargau, Karl Barth and his family left Switzerland for Germany and the endeavours of academic life.

3

Göttingen and Münster

Professor Barth

When Barth arrived in Göttingen he was 35 years old. Although excited, he was filled with trepidation. Before instructing students in the minutiae of Reformed doctrine he would first have to instruct himself. 'I can now admit', he wrote in 1927, 'that at the time I did not even possess the Reformed confessional writings, and had certainly never read them, quite apart from other horrendous gaps in my knowledge.'[1] He had dabbled in Calvin's *Institutes* in an amateurish way during his time as an assistant minister in Geneva some 12 years previously, but being professor of Reformed theology was a different matter entirely. He knew, however, that he had something to say, while the second edition of the Romans commentary, which would be published early in 1922, was more Calvinistic than he realized at the time. He was also gratified to receive at the same juncture an honorary doctorate from Münster in recognition of his contribution to contemporary theology.

The next two years saw Barth immerse himself with extraordinary intensity in the riches of the Calvinistic faith. 'What do I do? I study,' he informed Eduard Thurneysen in January 1922. 'Chiefly the Reformation and everything connected with it.'[2] Not yet sufficiently confident to embark on a constructive dogmatics of his own, he began by teaching historical theology. For the winter semester of 1921–2 he took as his theme the Heidelberg Catechism, Germany's leading Calvinistic primer, written in 1543. In the following summer semester came a course

27

on Ulrich Zwingli, the Swiss Reformer, Calvin the (winter) semester after that, and an assessment of the Reformed confessions in the summer semester of 1923. Side by side with his historical studies Barth would provide expositional lectures on Ephesians, the Epistle of James, 1 Corinthians, Philippians, 1 John and the Sermon on the Mount. The course on the Reformed confessions would be followed by an exceedingly shrewd and insightful analysis of Schleiermacher, whom he still regarded as a giant of the Reformed Church despite having to reject nearly everything the great Berlin theologian had taught.

It was John Calvin, however, who would remain the benchmark:

> Calvin is a cataract, a primeval forest, a demonic power, something directly down from Himalaya, absolutely Chinese, strange, mythological; I lack completely the means, the suction cups, even to assimilate this phenomenon, not to speak of presenting it adequately ... I could gladly and profitably set myself down and spend all the rest of my life just with Calvin.[3]

His lecture style was more prosaic than his colourful correspondence with Thurneysen, but no less earnest: 'Being taught by Calvin means entering into dialogue with him, with Calvin as the teacher and ourselves as the students, he speaking, we doing our best to follow him and then – this is the crux of the matter – making our own response to what he says' (*TJC* 4). What attracted him in Calvin was his doctrinal acumen, his clarity of thought and the way in which he allowed the concept of God's sovereignty not to impede but to encourage human ethical endeavour. Whereas Luther's conviction concerning justification by faith alone emphasized the human appropriation of God's saving benefits, the Genevan Reformer centred everything on a dynamic notion of deity that encompassed rather than overwhelmed the recipients' obedient response. For Barth, Calvin was a teacher of ethics as well as being an exponent of God's free and electing grace.

The theology of crisis

The preface to the second edition of *The Epistle to the Romans*, written in Safenwil in the previous September but appearing only now, contained a pugnacious refutation of the book's earlier critics and a powerful apologia for the integrity of this newly minted theology of God's Word. In what was a studied exaggeration, Barth claimed that 'the original has been so completely rewritten . . . that no stone remains in its old place' (*Ep. Rom.* 2). What was different was the rather confrontational tone in the second edition and its more uncompromising style: its content and thrust remained the same. To those who had claimed that the volume had been too overtly theological at the expense of being an exercise in textual scholarship: 'I do not want readers of this book to be under any illusions. They must expect nothing but theology' (*Ep. Rom.* 4). For the sophisticates who mocked its use of dialectic in favour of a spurious simplicity: 'Thirty years hence we may perhaps speak of simplicity, but now let us speak of the truth' (*Ep. Rom.* 5). For those who thought Barth disparaged scholarly criticism: 'I have nothing whatever to say against historical criticism. I recognize it, and once more state quite definitely that it is both necessary and justified' (*Ep. Rom.* 6). His complaint was against the sort of biblical criticism that had nothing useful to say about God. This had never been true of the scholarly theologians of the classical era. Calvin, for instance, having first established what stood in the text, set himself to rethink the whole material and to wrestle with it until the walls that separated the sixteenth century from the first became transparent. True theology, claimed Barth, was more than 'the mere deciphering of words' (*Ep. Rom.* 7). Despite his only recent acceptance into the guild, the junior Göttingen professor was withering in his critique of the practitioners of a merely academic theology: 'Is it that these learned men, for whose learning and erudition I have such genuine respect, fail to recognize the existence of any real substance at all, of any underlying problem, of any Word in the words?' (*Ep. Rom.* 9). 'Intelligent comment', he insisted, 'means that I am driven on till I stand with nothing before me but the enigma of the matter' (*Ep. Rom.* 8).

As well as being fully exercised in mastering his sources, Barth found himself having to explain and defend his theological stance. Semester breaks were hardly vacations, and in a series of lectures delivered in various places between the middle of and late 1922 he commended the new theology as best he could. A July address, 'The need and promise of Christian preaching', was a striking evocation of the preacher's dilemma: 'What is preaching?, not *how* does one do it but how *can* it be done?' (*WGWM*, 'Christian preaching' 97–135 [103]). The preacher was only human but the Word of God was divine. The only possibility was that God, in the event of self-revelation, would take up the preacher's discourse and make it his own. The Word of God was a negation, humanly speaking a paradox and an impossibility, yet only this could instil confidence and hope: 'Though we may have understood this a thousand times, it is still impossible to understand' (*WGWM*, 'Christian preaching' 119). Like John the Baptist in Matthias Grünewald's great medieval altarpiece at Isenheim, all the preacher could do was bear witness to Christ and point to that event: 'The whole situation of the Church suddenly becomes intelligible if it is seen as the framework of *this* event' (*WGWM*, 'Christian preaching' 123).

A second address, 'The problem of ethics today', delivered by Barth in September just as the course he had given on Calvin had come to an end, challenged those who had criticized the new theology for making ethics arbitrary and a given moral code impossible to sustain. His disdain for what he called 'the generation of 1914' was total (*WGWM*, 'Ethics' 136–82 [144]). Its philosophical tragedy had been its subjectivism and its unwitting thraldom to the cult of the autonomous will. Ethics were certainly possible, not according to a spurious Kantian neutrality, a specious notion of 'objectivity', but in response to the fact that God had actively elected humankind to a covenant relationship with himself: 'Since there is such a thing as forgiveness, which is always forgiveness of *sin*, there is such a thing as human conduct which is justified' (*WGWM*, 'Ethics' 172). Civilization, politics, even religion itself, could flourish not as some sort of sacred duty or as God's special ordinances of creation, but as simple witness to God's will in the coming of his kingdom. The divine action relativized human acts, setting people free to practise their obedience in the earthly sphere. This, Barth believed, was at the heart of Calvin's concept of the ethics of obedience.

A third address, 'The Word of God and the task of ministry', delivered in October 1922, was especially effective in showing the nature of Barth's dialectic method. Dialectic, or the use of two apparently contradictory truths in order to throw light on the illusive quality of reality, could all too easily become just one more technique to gain access to God. Were this to happen, even dialectic would come under the curse: 'There is no way from us to God – not even a *via negativa* – not even a *via dialectica* nor *paradoxa*. The god who stood at the end of some human way – even of this way – would not be God' (*WGWM*, 'Ethics' 177). The biblical God, however, active in self-revelation, did, in fact, reveal himself in a hidden and oblique way. 'As ministers we ought to speak of God. We are human, however, and so cannot speak of God. We ought therefore to recognize both *our obligation and our inability* and by that very recognition give God the glory' (*WGWM*, 'Ministry' 183–207 [186]).

By now Barth's theology, and that of his circle, was becoming widely known as the 'dialectical theology' or the 'theology of crisis', and its characteristic emphases were becoming familiar: 'One can *not* speak of God simply by speaking of man in a loud voice . . . There *is* no faculty in man through which revelation can be apprehended' (*WGWM*, 'Ministry' 196, 197). The euphoric response that these lectures provoked, though gratifying, also put enormous pressure on Barth, and it was little wonder that he complained of extreme overwork. As he wrote to Thurneysen in October 1922:

> Good heavens, how huge and varied Germany is! And there I am always, the inveterate traveller with my little briefcase . . . back and forth from the express to the D-train, in waiting rooms and on station platforms with a pipe that rarely goes out![4]

Between the Times

As the instigator of a dynamic theological movement, Barth found himself at the focal point of a new grouping of his peers. Their platform was a bimonthly journal entitled *Between the Times*, commenced in January 1923 and numbering among its contributors Thurneysen, Karl's brothers Peter and Heinrich, and Emil Brunner from Zürich, each of whom were fellow Swiss Reformed, and the German Lutherans Friedrich Gogarten and Rudolf Bultmann. Around the same time Barth had also encountered Paul Tillich, though the latter's interests even then were more cultural and philosophical than theological as such. Barth's renown, especially following the startling reception afforded the second edition of the Romans commentary, was to him bewildering. As he wrote in 1927:

> As I look back on my way I see myself as a man feeling his way up the steps of a dark church tower. By mistake he lays hold not of the hand rail but a bell rope and he has to listen, to his horror, to the great bell tolling above for everyone to hear.   (*DE* ix[5])

The intention was to write a commentary on an epistle by the apostle Paul. The result, much to Barth's genuine surprise, was the seeming reorientation of modern Protestant theology as a whole.

In Germany the winter of 1922–3 was severe. The economic situation was dire, with galloping inflation and the ensuing hardship was widespread. Barth was appalled by the apparent ineptitude of Germany's fledgling democratic government, though he was equally incensed by France's seizure of the heavily industrialized Ruhr in January 1923 as a reprisal after Germany failed to fulfil reparation payments demanded by the Versailles Treaty. He was, however, deeply uncomfortable with the chauvinistic nationalism of his Göttingen colleagues, from whom he was becoming more alienated by the day. By this time he was back in the classroom learning about Zwingli, his fellow Swiss, and sharing his freshly acquired knowledge with his students before embarking on a more satisfying study of the Reformation confessions. His expositional lectures on 1 Corinthians would appear as *The Resurrection of the Dead* in 1924.

Along with these academic tasks, between January and May 1923 he was involved in a courteous but uncompromising altercation with Adolf von Harnack, the esteemed Berlin church historian, in the pages of Martin Rade's *The Christian World*. Perturbed by the new theology, Harnack had penned 'Fifteen theses to the despisers of scientific theology'. Although Barth was not mentioned by name, it was obvious that he was the target. The younger man responded immediately with 'Fifteen answers to Professor Adolf von Harnack', which led to an open letter by Harnack, a more lengthy response by Barth, and a postscript provided by Harnack. Although the discourse was measured, there was no doubt about the depth of the divide. For Harnack, scientific theology entailed the study of Christian religion according to the norms of Enlightenment rationality. For Barth, Christian theology could only be truly scientific when it functioned in the light of its own criteria, namely, the unique self-revelation of the triune God. This, for Harnack, was a throwback to a pre-critical age: 'I do sincerely regret that the answers to my questions only point to the magnitude of the gap that divides us.'[6] Barth would not yield an inch: 'My rejoinder . . . is that you empty faith by asserting a continuity between the "human" and faith just as you empty revelation by saying there is continuity between history and revelation.'[7] As liberal theology could only envisage Christ, faith and the resurrection in naturalistic terms, the gospel had been emasculated and stripped of its scandal. As well as there being a generational divide (Harnack was 71 and Barth 36), it was obvious that one movement was passing and another taking its place. There was little common ground between the generation of 1914 and a vigorous and youthful theology of the Word of God.

The Göttingen Dogmatics

The year 1924 would become another highly productive one. In class Barth found himself in stimulating if critical dialogue with Schleiermacher, expounding 1 John and preparing at last to embark on a constructive dogmatics of his own. A compendium of his most important articles appeared as *The Word of God and Theology* (its 1928 English translation would be entitled *The Word of God and the Word of Man*), along with a volume of sermons, jointly authored with Thurneysen, entitled *Come, Holy Spirit!* Of more lasting significance, though ostensibly hidden to Barth's public at the time, was his proficient attempt at composing a whole dogmatic scheme. Begun in the summer of 1924 and spread over three semesters, he would provide for his students a complete systematic theology. Intentionally echoing Calvin's *Institutio Christianae Religionis*, or *Institutes*, his 'Instruction in the Christian Religion', otherwise known as the *Göttingen Dogmatics*, would provide an assessment of revelation, Scripture and the preached Word in semester one, the doctrines of God and humanity in semester two, concluding with Christology, reconciliation and eschatology in semester three.

The *Göttingen Dogmatics*, which remained unpublished during his lifetime, would provide a breakthrough for Barth as a constructive theologian rather than merely confirm his status as an *enfant terrible*, and it would remain the basis for his momentous *Church Dogmatics*, begun nearly a decade later.

> I shall never forget the spring vacation of 1924. I sat in my study in Göttingen, faced with the task of giving lectures on dogmatics for the first time. Not for a long time could anyone have been as plagued as I was at that time by the question, could I do it? . . . I saw myself, so to speak, without a teacher, alone in the wide open spaces.[8]

It was one thing to point to the weaknesses of liberalism (and conventional conservative orthodoxy); his task now was to put something better in its place. On the basis of convictions that had been spelled out in the Romans commentary, Barth knew that he would have to begin with the concept of God's radical self-revelation in Christ. This meant that he would be forced back to the doctrine of the Trinity: 'Everything indeed depends on *this* denominator,' he told Thurneysen in March 1924. 'A Trinity of *being*, not just an economic Trinity! At all costs the doctrine of Trinity!'[9]

For generations the doctrine of the Trinity had been either a conundrum or a commonplace within Protestant theology, but for Barth it had now become a luminously relevant truth. If revelation came wholly from God and it did so only in Christ, Christ *must* share deity with the Father to the full. And if human beings were to know Christ immediately and not just derivatively as the bearer of God's exclusive revelation, they could only do so through the Holy Spirit. This implied that the Spirit too shared full deity with the Father and the Son. This was not sophistry or intellectualism but a clear inference from the truth of revelation. Yet God was not merely divine in virtue of his self-revelation; God possessed deity in and of himself: 'All of this, seen in this light,' he ruminated to Thurneysen, 'seems to have its own good sense. I understand the Trinity as the *problem of the inalienable subjectivity of God in his revelation.*'[10] Soon, to his amazement, he would be championing the doctrines of the deity of Christ, the impersonal nature of Christ's unique humanity, the virgin birth and a rash of truths thought to have been unserviceable since the beginning of the modern era.

> After much racking of my brains and astonishment I have finally to acknowledge that orthodoxy is right on almost all points, and to hear myself saying things in lectures which neither as a student nor as a Safenwil pastor would I ever have dreamed could really be so.[11]

Barth had been helped immeasurably by a collection of classical Reformed texts edited by the nineteenth-century scholar Heinrich Heppe: 'Out of date, dusty, unattractive, almost like a table of logarithms, dreary to read, stiff and eccentric on almost every page I opened.'[12] Yet having the grace to persevere, he soon found that this collection gave him the material he needed with which to refashion a startlingly new though mature theology that was in accord with the genius of a sorely neglected past: 'We are a generation that has to learn again . . . what are the presuppositions that a Thomas [Aquinas], an Augustine before him, and a Calvin after him could quietly take for granted' (*GD* 4). Although inspired by the profound seriousness and ecclesial gravity of the tradition, Barth was never tempted merely to restate Calvinism in a modern guise. He was acutely aware that his generation's questions could never be answered in a naive, traditionalist or pre-critical way. What he found in the post-Reformation Calvinism was not a golden age but a resource with which to do theology that was both deeply traditional and strikingly novel. The *Göttingen Dogmatics* would prove that it could be done.

Karl Barth's status in Göttingen as an honorary rather than a full professor was precarious, while his relations with his colleagues had been strained from the outset. When an opportunity came to leave, he took it eagerly. In the summer of 1925 the Protestant faculty at Münster, which had already awarded him a doctorate, proposed him for its chair in theology and New Testament exegesis, and by October he had left Göttingen for good. He was serenaded by his students in a torchlight procession on the night before his departure, much to the disapproval of his soon-to-be-erstwhile colleagues. Some months later, the family joined him in their new home. By then Karl and Nelly had a fifth child, Hans-Jakob.

Encounter with Catholicism

If Göttingen had been Lutheran, the city of Münster, capital of Westphalia, was Catholic, and Barth soon found himself not only enjoying more congenial company but interacting for the first time with theologians of the Catholic Church. His work in Münster included a remarkably detailed lecture series on more recent religious thought that would eventually appear as *Protestant Theology in the Nineteenth Century*, exegetical lectures on the Gospel of John, Colossians and Philippians, the latter being published as a commentary in 1927, along with regular seminars on Calvin's *Institutes* and works by Schleiermacher and Ritschl. Seminars on *Cur Deus Homo?* by the medieval Anselm of Canterbury, and on Thomas Aquinas's *Summa Theologica*, reflected his growing fascination with the theology of the Catholic Church.

A milestone, however, was the appearance in late 1927 of his first published systematic theology, *The Christian Dogmatics in Outline*. Building on the *Göttingen Dogmatics* and not radically different from the first volume of the *Church Dogmatics* that would be issued in 1932, it explained Barth's concept of the Word of God as a basis for theology. Its author was not wholly confident in the work. Describing it as 'coming from the pen of a beginner', Barth was afraid that he was merely replicating a version of orthodoxy rather than doing justice to the dynamic reality of God's self-disclosure in Christ (*DE* v). It was written by 'a younger man to younger men' – Barth was, in fact, 41 at the time – in order to provide a more finished structure to the building he had begun to erect a decade earlier (*DE* vi). A growing sense of distance between himself and the contemporaries who were

37

now publishing regularly in *Between the Times* made him progressively more uncomfortable with the wording, if not the substance, of the volume. He now felt he had been too superficial in his account of the proclamation of the Word of God. He saw that the work suggested, perhaps, that the Word of God was dependent for its effectiveness on an analysis of human existence rather than being in a sovereign manner free. Unwilling to allow this perception to stand, Barth would relaunch his dogmatic project with the *Church Dogmatics* five years later.

Undoubtedly, however, it was his interaction with Roman Catholic theologians that gave Barth the most satisfaction. A series of key lectures, dialogue with colleagues in the university's Catholic faculty and the company of Erich Przywara, a Jesuit from Munich who introduced him to the concept of the *analogia entis*, or 'analogy of being', sharpened both his appreciation for Catholic theology and for the reasons the Reformers had rejected it so squarely. The *analogia entis* was the idea of a natural affinity between God and humankind that provided the basis for God's imparting through the sacraments of infused grace. His dispute with Catholicism paralleled his rejection of Protestant liberalism; it allowed a human mediator, in this case the Church, to threaten God's absolute sovereignty in Christ. There was but one Church, holy, catholic and apostolic, of which both Catholics and Protestants claimed to be a part. The existence of the papal ministry or a sacrificial priesthood were secondary matters; the primary concern had to do with an apparent mastery over grace: he claimed, 'The Church does not have control of its unity . . . The Church does not control its holiness' (*T&C*, 'Church' 272–85 [283]). All the Church could do was to heed, not possess, the Word: 'The Church does not control its catholicity; the eternal, omnipresent God controls it' (*T&C*, 'Church' 284). Faith can never be a possession vouchsafed by a sacramental system, only a sovereign free gift perpetually offered and ever calling forth a dynamic and continual response. Similarly, the revelation of God's holiness along with the unity, the catholicity and

apostolic nature of the Church was not a given, a static ontological state to which the Church could lay claim. These, too,
were gifts that had continually to be affirmed in faith.

There was no doubt in Barth's mind that the Roman Catholic
Church posed a formidable challenge to modern Protestantism:
'It has kept at least the claim to the knowledge of the substance
[of the faith] and has guarded it . . . The substance may perhaps
be distorted but it is not lost!' (*T&C*, 'Roman Catholicism'
307–33 [314, 315]). That was hardly the case with a truncated,
watered down liberal modernism. Were he to be convinced that
the religion of Schleiermacher or Ritschl was the inevitable
outcome of the Protestant Reformation, Barth would have
no option but to quit the Evangelical Church and become a
Catholic. That, however, did not have to happen. What was
essential was a return to the Pauline gospel of an imparted, not
an infused grace, which had been so pointedly rediscovered by
the Reformers: 'Calvin and Luther are by no means a spent
force' (*HG&CL* 70). By confusing justification and sanctification,
both human sinfulness and the divine mercy had been relativized: 'According to the doctrine of Trent, the fall of man from
God does not affect the centre of his nature, his real being, but
produces only a weakening and warping of his free, original
good will' (*T&C*, 'Roman Catholicism' 327). Such a confusion
went beyond the sixteenth-century Council of Trent and back
to the earliest decades of the Latin Church. Barth's 1929 lecture
series, *The Holy Ghost and the Christian Life,* was a frontal attack
on the Augustinian confusion of justification with sanctification
that was at the root of the Roman Catholic scheme. Quoting
copiously from the Reformers, Barth aligned his own dialectical teaching on the sovereign freedom of the Word with the
magisterial doctrines of Calvin and Luther:

> The Christian is *simul peccator et justus*, and the surmount-
> ing of this irreconcilable contradiction does not lie in the
> Christian – not even in the most secret sanctum of his

existence, nor does it happen in any of the hours of his life's journey, not even in those hours most moved and profound, of conversion and death – but it is the action of the Word of God, the action of Christ, who is always the One who makes him out to be a sinner, in order to make him, though a sinner, into a righteous man.

(*HG&CL* 52–3)

'Aunt Lollo'

In the late summer of 1929 Barth was approached by Bonn with a view to his taking up the position of professor of systematic theology there that would become vacant the following year. Although much happier at Münster than he had been at Göttingen, he was ready to move to what was a more distinguished faculty and a more senior chair. Three years earlier he had made the acquaintance of Charlotte von Kirschbaum, a 27-year-old nurse much involved in Lutheran Church circles, who had been drawn to Barth's theology and would soon be drawn to Barth himself. The attraction would be mutual. Through the offices of George Merz, Charlotte's pastor and a friend of Barth, she became his research assistant and secretary, and would soon become indispensible in his work. The exact nature of the relationship remains a matter of speculation, but there is no doubt that it caused tension in the household, for Nelly in particular, and would be the source of veiled consternation for the next three decades.[13] 'Aunt Lollo', as she would become known to the Barth children, would remain unswerving in her dedication to Barth and his project, and from 1929 virtually a member of the family. This, in turn, would cause Karl, Nelly and Charlotte herself not inconsiderable suffering and pain. 'But the work of theology was joyful', reported Rose Marie Oswald, later to become Barth's daughter-in-law, 'and the involvement in that work, to whatever extent, held the three together through toils and perils.'[14]

4

The Bonn years

Discovering Anselm

Karl Barth's final semester in Münster was the winter one of 1929–30. Having accepted the Bonn chair in October, he would commence work there the following spring. The political situation was precarious. There were enormous tensions among the people, and the fissures ran deep. Again Barth was bitterly disappointed that too many conformist academics seemed to want to sabotage the liberal Weimar republic, post-war Germany's ill-fated experimental democracy. Like the vast majority of progressives, Barth found it difficult to take the extreme right wing, with its demagogic leader, Adolf Hitler, seriously. As he admitted later, 'I was utterly wrong at the time in seeing no danger in the rise of National Socialism, which had already begun.'[1] For him, this rise was more absurd than sinister, and even though he would soon rue his own naivety, he would still find himself in a minority, ever the Swiss Calvinist among a triumphalistic and seemingly unstoppable Lutheran nationalism.

Barth's immediate concern was to his calling as a theologian of the Word of God. By now his reputation was secure and he could even relish an element of theological stardom. Barth's lectures were packed to the doors and so popular were his seminars that they had to be restricted to students who had passed a qualifying test. Theology in Bonn had never been so popular, and the reason was Karl Barth. He was also by now drawing students from abroad. As the Scot John McConnachie wrote:

To sit in his classroom as the writer has done, and see
and hear him among the students who hang upon his
lips, to be with him in the more intimate surroundings of
his seminars and at the open evenings in his own home,
where he lets himself go, is to recognize that he is not only
a great theological teacher but one of the spiritual forces
of the day.[2]

Since his turn to historical theology at Göttingen, and even
more so since his dialogue with Roman Catholicism at Münster,
Barth had spent more and more time studying the theologians
of the early or patristic Church and those of the medieval West.
He had already taken Anselm's *Cur Deus Homo?* ('Why did God
become human?') as his seminar text during his first semester
in Bonn, and was now determined to clarify his own method
by reflecting on Anselm's so-called 'proof' for the existence of
God. That proof was found in the medieval theologian's
Proslogion, but in fact, argued Barth, it was no proof in the
ordinary sense at all: God's existence could never be proved
by a process of human deduction, it could only be believed.
It was God who proved his own existence by revealing
himself to humankind. This God had already done in Christ,
who could only be known in any immediate sense through
the Holy Spirit – in other words, through God himself. God
was always the divine subject. In Christ, however, he had made
himself accessible to men and women, though always retaining his sovereign freedom. Anselm's 'proof' took the form of
a prayer. In it he did not ask God for knowledge on which to
base his (human) conclusion that there was a God. Rather he
asked in faith how God's already given revelation should be
understood. All human rationality could do was to respond to
the revelation that had already been granted.

This, for Barth, was no new insight. It was there, in dialectical form, in the Romans commentary and had been worked
out with surprising alacrity in the *Göttingen Dogmatics* and

the *Christian Dogmatics*. What was new was the affirmation that this too had been the case with the twelfth-century Anselm, previously thought to have championed 'natural theology', namely, a theology rooted not in God's free self-revelation in Christ but in people's ability to reason themselves into believing in God. The volume *Anselm: Fides Quaerens Intellectum* ('Anselm: Faith Seeking Understanding'), completed in the summer of 1931, was clearly important for the way in which Barth perceived his own development: 'In these years I have had to rid myself of the last remnants of a philosophical . . . foundation and exposition of Christian doctrine,' he reported in 1938.

> The real document of this farewell is . . . the book about the evidence for God in Anselm of Canterbury which appeared in 1931. Among all my books I regard this as the one written with the greatest satisfaction . . . For before, I had been at least partly hampered, not so much by church tradition, as by the eggshells of philosophical systematics.
>
> (*HICMM* 42–4)

However important, in retrospect, Barth felt the Anselm book to be, a far more significant occasion was the appearance of the first volume of *Church Dogmatics* I, *The Doctrine of the Word of God*. *Church Dogmatics* I/1, first presented as lectures in the summer semester of 1931 and concluded two semesters later, contained the first half of his mature doctrine of the Word of God. Following 50 pages of introduction, it included a 200-page first chapter, 'The Word of God as the criterion of dogmatics', and another 200-page half-chapter entitled 'The revelation of God; Part 1: The triune God', which would be concluded in *Church Dogmatics* I/2 in 1938. Its translator, the Scottish theologian G. T. Thomson, wrote in his Introduction that the volume constituted 'undoubtedly the greatest treatise on the Trinity since the Reformation' (*DWG* iii–v [v]). *Church Dogmatics* I/1 will be discussed in the next chapter.

Theological Existence Today!

Barth's becoming the focus of enormous interest in Bonn had the effect of making the differences between him and his contemporaries more glaring, though with Thurneysen, who had been appointed minister of Basel Cathedral in 1929, there was complete unanimity: 'I may take it as well known that there exists between Eduard Thurneysen and myself a theological affinity which is of long standing and has always shown itself to be self-evident' (*CD* I/1 xiv–v). Not so with Rudolf Bultmann, Friedrich Gogarten or Barth's fellow Swiss, Emil Brunner. Bultmann, primarily a New Testament scholar, was keen to utilize existentialist categories in order to make biblical material contemporary, while Gogarten was being drawn to the notion of an innate law within the human soul as a presupposition for accepting the gospel message. These differences surfaced in the late 1920s, though it was not until 1933 that the rupture would occur publicly: Gogarten, a nationalistic Lutheran in sympathy with the current renewal spearheaded by Hitler, would state that God's law was identical with the law of the German people. Barth, who had already disassociated himself from Gogarten's theology, erupted, and in a ferocious article in the October 1933 edition of *Between the Times* stated that the theology of the Word of God was wholly incompatible with any concept of natural, or German, religiosity. The article spelled the demise of the magazine. Although Barth's relations with Bultmann (who would never capitulate to Nazism) remained cordial, his disagreement with his existentializing theology remained profound:

> From my standpoint all of you . . . represent a large-scale return to the fleshpots of Egypt. If I am not deceived, all of you . . . are trying to understand faith as a human possibility, and therefore you are once again surrendering theology to philosophy.[3]

This, for Barth, was to jeopardize all that the new theology had achieved. It would mean a recrudescence of liberalism and a return to a failed past.

On 30 January 1933 Hitler came to power in Berlin. Such was the assimilation of German Protestantism into mainstream German culture that most church people were unaware of the implications of Nazi ideology for Christian faith. The challenge for Karl Barth was to maintain the integrity of the biblical revelation and allow God's righteous judgement in the gospel to show Nazism up for what it was. After having published on the axiomatic nature of the first commandment, 'You shall have no other gods before me' (Exodus 20.3; Deuteronomy 5.7) in March, in a treatise written in a single sitting at the end of June – *Theological Existence Today!* – he issued a blistering attack on the growing compromise between conventional Protestantism and the current regime:

> Under the stormy assault of principalities, powers and rulers of this world's darkness, we seek for God elsewhere than in his Word, and seek his Word somewhere else than in Jesus Christ, and seek Jesus Christ elsewhere than in the Holy Scriptures of the Old and New Testaments.
>
> (*TET* 15)

In a way the political situation was inconsequential. The Church's task was to be true to the gospel in whatever circumstances it found itself. The pamphlet was aimed partially at the so-called 'German Christians', a Nazi-inspired caucus within the state Church who demanded that Christianity should be assimilated into the Nazi system, that the autonomy of each of Germany's regional Churches, the *Landeskirchen*, should be forfeited in the name of national unity, and that the new National Church should implement the 'Führer Principle', namely, leadership under one single leader, the 'Reich Bishop', who would swear personal allegiance to Adolf Hitler. Barth's invective was volcanic: 'The veriest tyro in theology knows

that with their thinking we are already with a small collection
of odds and ends from the great theological dustbins of the
despised eighteenth and nineteenth centuries' (*TET* 53). The
problem again was a theology of nature, not of grace, of
human religiosity and not the divine Word, of the spirituality
of a diffuse, this-worldly immanence and not the unique
revelation of God in Jesus Christ. As Barth recalled:

> I still had nothing essentially new to say. At that time
> I said rather just what I had always tried to say, namely,
> that beside God we can have no other gods, that the
> Holy Spirit . . . is enough to guide the church in all truth,
> and that the grace of Jesus Christ is all-sufficient for the
> forgiveness of our sins and the ordering of our lives.
>
> (*HICMM* 46)

It was the context that had made this message revolutionary.
Revelation had occurred in Jesus Christ, God's sovereign authority was absolute, natural theology was a heresy and the Church's
faith was derived from the Holy Scriptures and not from human
history, no matter how momentous it may seem. There could
be no compromise between the Word of God and the alien
ideologies of a worldly power: 'Without my wanting it, or doing
anything to facilitate it, this had of necessity to take on the
character of a summons, a challenge, a battle cry, a confession'
(*HICMM* 46). The first blast of the German 'Church Struggle'
had been sounded.

The Church Struggle was the countermovement, led by the
Lutheran pastor Martin Niemöller, to prevent state law, now
infected by Nazi ideology, from being enacted within the state
Churches. It was fuelled by a reaction to the growing popularity
of the German Christians and the realization, following a
notorious rally in the Berlin sports arena in November 1933,
that Nazism was in essence an anti-Semitic pagan pseudo-
religion and as such wholly incompatible with the Christian
faith. By early 1934 the 'Confessing Church', an association of

pastors and congregations who had pledged loyalty to Christ according to the Protestant confessions, found themselves unexpectedly at the forefront of opposition to the regime. The resistance was sectional and muted: few Confessing pastors realized the gravity of the political situation – in contrast to the church situation – and were even less scandalized by the scapegoating of the Jews. But for all its limitations, the Confessing Church did at least offer a real challenge to state rule.

The Church's first national synod was scheduled for late May, at Barmen in the city of Wuppertal. In preparation, Barth and two others were commissioned to write a theological declaration setting out the basis of the Confessionalists' creed. As it transpired, Barth became virtually the sole author of the Barmen Declaration, the boldest statement of Christ's sole authority over the Church to have emerged since the Reformation:

> Jesus Christ, as he is attested to us in Holy Scripture, is the one Word of God, whom we have to hear and whom we have to trust and obey in life and in death.
>
> We condemn as false doctrine that the Church can and must recognize as God's revelation other events and powers, forms and truths, apart from and alongside this one Word of God.   (*CD* II/1 172)

Ostensibly a platform for the Confessing Church's opposition to the Nazification of the Church, it was in effect a manifestation of Barth's theology of the Word at its most uncompromising. For Barth, Nazism was only a symptom of the disease. At its root was the pernicious concept of a natural theology, independent of God's sole revelation in Christ.

No!

It was this context that provided the poignancy for Barth's painful rift with Emil Brunner, his fellow Swiss Calvinist: 'In the midst of the German Church Struggle there occurred the most dramatic theological controversy of our age.'[4] Brunner, already aggrieved at being criticized in *Church Dogmatics* I/1, issued a prickly rejoinder early in 1934 entitled *Nature and Grace*. In it he taunted Barth for his one-sidedness and defended the view that the Bible did allow for a natural theology of its own. The concept of the *imago Dei*, or image of God, in humankind, individuals' moral consciousness, the idea of 'common grace' as opposed to special or saving grace, the ordinances of creation including marriage and the state, 'the point of contact' or human beings' natural receptivity to the gospel call – all these pointed towards a natural knowledge of God that opened the way for the Word, when heard, to be affirmed. Brunner had devised an apologetic scheme – eristics – based on this natural receptivity to God, which served as a preparation for a more complete revelation in the Word. 'I am still of the opinion that there should be an eristic theology based upon this knowledge,'[5] he claimed. 'It is the task of our theological generation to find the way back to a true *theologia naturalis*.'[6] With mystifying naivety, Brunner still believed that he and Barth were in effect saying the same thing, and that all that his colleague needed to do was return to Calvin's own concept of natural theology and a truer doctrine of God's Word.

Barth was mortified by Brunner's strictures, coming as they did from long-democratic Switzerland, while within the Church in Germany there was a battle with Nazism being waged to the death. On the one hand, he felt that the views of Brunner, who was said to be a theologian of the Word, were staggeringly perverse, and on the other, that his timing was wholly inept. He responded angrily in a counter-pamphlet entitled simply *No!*: 'The doctrine of the point of contact and the whole of Brunner's teaching on nature and grace . . . has to be most categorically opposed on the score that it is incompatible with the third article of the creed.'[7] The Holy Spirit, claimed Barth, does not stand in need of any point of contact apart from the one God himself creates. That there is a point of contact is not in dispute, just as the existence of humankind in God's image can be said to be analogous to the existence of God, but neither of these facts could be discovered independently of God's own sovereign revelation of himself: 'Only retrospectively is it possible to reflect on the way in which he makes contact with man, and this retrospect will ever be a retrospect upon a *miracle*.'[8]

Barth, technically a civil servant in the employment of the state, was required to swear an oath of loyalty to Hitler, by now both chancellor and president of Germany. This he had refused to do, just as he had refused resolutely to begin his lectures with the Hitler salute, choosing instead a Scripture reading and to have his students sing a hymn. Suspension from his post was only a matter of time. It occurred on 26 November 1934, the drama being described vividly by another of his foreign students, the Welshman Ivor Oswy Davies.

> A great crowd gathered together and nervous anticipation filled the air. I saw from the back of the hall, unusually, the small band of grey-shirted theological students who were zealous for Hitler . . . They glared at the rest of us, who supported Professor Barth, like birds of prey. It was clear that their only role was to provide support for the vice-chancellor in the execution of his shameful deed.

Davies described how the vice-chancellor entered the hall nervously and told the assembled students why his most renowned professor was being dismissed. The crowd stamped their feet and jeered as he left. 'It only lasted ten minutes but it will be etched on my memory forever. For there, in that ritual of darkness, I witnessed the University of Bonn losing its very soul.'[9] Although Barth appealed against the decision, the suspension was upheld.

Unclear as to the next step, Karl busied himself in early 1935 with preaching, guest-lecturing and giving Bible classes for his erstwhile students at his home, though even these activities ceased when, in March, he was banned from public speaking. Still allowed to travel, in late spring he visited Holland and Switzerland. In June 1935 Bonn served him with a final notice to quit. Basel, knowing of his predicament, invited him to take up a specially created chair in theology, and within days Barth and his family had moved to the city of his birth. Karl was 49 years old. Apart from one clandestine visit late in the year he would not return to Germany until 1946, by which time Bonn lay in ruins.

Church Dogmatics

The next four years, between Barth's return to Switzerland and the outbreak of the Second World War, would see him supporting the Confessing Church as best he could and continuing with his own theological project. A visit to Geneva in 1936, where he contributed to the jubilee celebrations for the Reformation, was especially fruitful. Listening to a paper on the doctrine of election by his friend, the French Reformed pastor Pierre Maury, stimulated his thinking enormously. By rooting the concept of election wholly in Christ, the covenant partner of humankind, Maury shifted the focus from God's inscrutable decree whereby some were saved and others were damned, towards God's gracious will for the whole of humankind. Barth felt that this did more justice to the thrust of Pauline theology, and in his Gifford Lectures, delivered at Aberdeen in 1937–8, he developed this theme. Basing his treatment on John Knox's Scots Confession of 1560, he argued that God was not just the sovereign Lord, rather God had acted in his very essence in order to be for and with humankind: 'The Reformed Church and Reformed theology have never spoken about God and man as if God were everything and man were nothing. That is a caricature of Reformed teaching' (*KGSG* 35). God as Creator presupposes a creation in which God has chosen to be bounteous and merciful. Moreover, God has done this from eternity in Christ: 'Let us proceed from the simple fact that in the revelation of God in Jesus Christ, God and man meet, and therefore are really together' (*KGSG* 36). In Christ, humankind becomes not God's antithesis or his servant, still less his slave, but his covenant partner and cohort. Humankind too possesses glory.

Man, of course, as the gospel had always claimed, is still a sinner. There is no room for any Enlightenment optimism as to human perfectibility; humankind is under judgement and the object of the divine wrath. But there is something more central to disobedience and condemnation, namely, that God has chosen *for* humankind:

> That man is *against* God is true and important and has to
> be taken seriously. But what is ever truer, *more* important
> and to be taken *more* seriously is the other fact that God
> in Jesus Christ is *for* man.   (*KGSG* 46)

This is not fortuitous; it has nothing to do with man as man; man is sinner and as such is damned, his will is in bondage and the *imago Dei* has been hopelessly marred. In no way can sin be downplayed. Yet God is for humankind because God has chosen, or elected, to be so. Election is no abstraction, neither does it have to do with two distinct groups, the reprobate and the saved. It has, rather, to do with Adam, the whole human race, and even more basically with the Second Adam, Jesus Christ:

> God's eternal decree and man's election and thus the whole
> of what is called the doctrine of predestination cannot but
> be misunderstood unless it is understood in its connection
> with the truth of the divine–human nature of Jesus Christ.
>   (*KGSG* 77)

This was a huge breakthrough in the understanding of election, and would be worked out in detail in *Church Dogmatics* II/2 in 1942.

Church Dogmatics I/2 was published early in 1938 and included Barth's powerful treatment of the Incarnation of the Word, the outpouring of the Holy Spirit, the doctrine of Scripture and the proclamation of the Church. The year itself would prove momentous. By September, Hitler had annexed Czechoslovakia. Barth was appalled by free Europe's, and Switzerland's, appeasement of a brutal and tyrannical regime. More and more he found himself drawn towards political protest. Not least of his concerns was the fate of the Jews. 'Anyone who is in principle hostile to the Jews', he declared, 'must also be seen as in principle an enemy of Jesus Christ. Anti-Semitism is a sin against the Holy Spirit.'[10] By September 1939, for the second time in less than three decades, Europe found itself at war.

Between 1939 and 1945, Barth, now confined to Switzerland, worked assiduously on his doctrine of God. *Church Dogmatics* II/1, *The Doctrine of God*, covering the knowledge of God and the reality of God, appeared in 1939, and volume II/2, on election and ethics, was published in 1942. The next two chapters will provide an overview of their main themes.

5

The doctrine of the Word of God

Introduction

Church Dogmatics I/1 (1932) and I/2 (1938) form the basis for Barth's mature doctrine of the Word of God. The argument is cumulative rather than linear, and although elaborate in detail and rhetorically sophisticated (and forceful), its general thrust is fairly straightforward. God, for Barth, is ever active; God has chosen to reveal himself in the Word, and it is only through the Word that God can be known.

Dogmatics, for Barth, occurs within the Church. It is the intellectual discipline wherein the Christian community scrutinizes its discourse concerning God. It is not a freestanding enterprise or a neutral affair, rather it operates within the relationship of faith. 'Dogmatics is quite impossible except as an act of faith, in the determination of human action by listening to Jesus Christ and as obedience to him' (*CD* I/1 17). Whereas Protestant modernism strove for a putative autonomy, an attitude of detached objectivity, evangelical dogmatics functions in response to God's unique self-disclosure in the Word. 'Dogmatics must always be undertaken as an act of penitence,' claims Barth. '[Without] prayer ... there can be no dogmatic work' (*CD* I/1 22–3).

Barth crosses swords at the outset with his colleagues Emil Brunner, Karl Heim (a Tübingen theologian keen to synthesize theology with the modern scientific outlook) and Rudolf Bultmann (see Chapter 4). Unlike the *Christian Dogmatics* and the *Göttingen Dogmatics* before that, Barth structured the

Church Dogmatics to include sometimes extensive blocks in smaller print in which he would dialogue with contemporaries, quote often copiously from patristic, medieval, Reformation and modern sources and expound biblical texts. These are almost invariably the most fascinating sections in the *Church Dogmatics* and frequently shed incandescent light on the discussion in hand. For Barth, Brunner was simply wrong-headed in seeking a 'point of contact' with secular man, while in positing human self-understanding as the key for a contemporary belief in Christ, Bultmann was guilty of succumbing to an alien philosophy that would in the end be inimical to the gospel. Barth's fear is that in these rather desperate apologetic stratagems the context will always overshadow the content. It was his immovable conviction that God's revelation was sufficient in itself:

> The place from which the way of dogmatic knowledge is to be ... understood can be neither a prior anthropological possibility nor a subsequent ecclesiastical reality, but only the present moment in the speaking and hearing of Jesus Christ himself, the divine creation of light in our hearts.
>
> (*CD* I/1 41)

Following his two paragraphs of introduction – 'paragraphs' in the *Church Dogmatics* are denoted by the symbol § and can extend over scores, sometimes hundreds, of pages; they are the principal divisions within the text through which the author develops his argument – Barth proceeds to expound 'the threefold form of the Word of God' and the way it can be known (§§ 4–6), which will lead to a quite remarkable account of the Trinitarian nature of God (§§ 8–12), magisterial in its insightfulness and majestic in its scope.

The threefold form of the Word of God

That God is dynamic, active, purposeful is presupposed throughout Barth's work, and what is true of God is true of God's

Word. The Word of God is never a possession, a human possibility or an aspect of our own religious genius, rather it is God's free and sovereign communication of himself. The threefold form of the Word is that of proclamation, Holy Scripture and what Barth refers to as 'the Word of God revealed'. As befitted a theologian of the Reformed Church, his ideal of preaching was exalted:

> Proclamation is human speech in and by which God himself speaks like a king through the mouth of his herald, and which is meant to be heard and accepted as speech in and by which God himself speaks, and therefore heard and accepted in faith as divine decision concerning life and death, as divine judgement and pardon, eternal law and eternal gospel both together.   (*CD* I/1 52)

The fact that a preacher proclaims a gospel message from a pulpit does not automatically mean that the event of revelation will occur. God retains his freedom even within the relationship of faith. 'Proclamation must ever and again *become* proclamation' (*CD* I/1 88, emphasis added), he claims. God and his revelation can never be taken for granted, presumed upon or controlled; they can only be accepted in anticipation and hope as a miracle and event: 'We have [revelation] as it gives itself to us or not at all' (*CD* I/1 91–2). God is eternally subject but, under the veil of the human preaching, God gives himself as an objective reality within the world. This being the case, listeners can be wholly confident that the Word of God *will* be heard. The objective character of this event is vouchsafed by the fact that God has promised to reveal himself when the Church's proclamation is in accordance with the biblical witness to Christ as Lord.

The second form of the Word of God is Holy Scripture. The Old Testament and the New witness to God's revelation in Christ, they correspond to that revelation but they cannot be directly equated with it: 'We do the Bible poor and unwelcome

honour if we equate it directly with . . . revelation itself' (*CD* I/1
112). Scripture, like preaching, is a human construct – as flawed,
limited and deficient as anything else. Nevertheless, it becomes
the medium whereby the infallible God once more conveys the
reality of himself. If Protestant orthodoxy thought of revelation
in terms of imparting propositions about God, and Catholic
theology depicted grace as an entity infused through the
sacramental channels of the Church, for Barth, reflecting, as
he believed, the conviction of Luther and Calvin, revelation
was nothing less than Christ giving himself in a dynamic
and personal way to his people. When the Church preaches a
message faithful to Scripture, it allows itself to become the locus
wherein the event of revelation occurs:

> When the Church hears this Word – and it is heard in the
> prophets and the apostles and nowhere else – it hears a
> magisterial and ultimate Word which it can never again
> confuse or place on a level with any other word.
>
> (*CD* I/1 108)

Although God retains his sovereign freedom, within the dynamic of revelation's miraculous self-giving, Scripture plays
its essential and unique part: 'The Bible is God's Word to the
extent that God causes it to be his Word, to the extent that he
speaks through it' (*CD* I/1 109). (The seemingly arbitrary nature
of this statement is qualified in *Church Dogmatics* I/2, where
Scripture's reliability as a canonical source is underscored.)

Both preaching and Scripture, in Barth, take the form of
witness. Like the huge index finger of John the Baptist in
Matthias Grünewald's depiction of the crucifixion in the
Isenheim altarpiece, the Church's proclamation and its Bible
point towards Christ: 'Revelation . . . does not differ from the
person of Jesus Christ nor from the reconciliation accomplished
in him' (*CD* I/1 119). This, in fact, is Barth's third form of the
Word, on which both preaching and Scripture depend. The
stupendous freedom of this act of redemptive revelation is

discussed in § 5, while Barth is insistent that human response is never overwhelmed or undercut by God's sovereign event but in fact is made possible by it. God's Word is knowable, indeed it can be experienced and felt. The tremendous polemic against a feeling-based pietism and Schleiermacher's theology of experience is, for the moment, put to one side. 'There can be no objection in principle to describing this event as "experience" and even as "religious experience",' he claimed. 'The quarrel is not with the term nor with the . . . thing the term might finally denote' (*CD* I/1 193), namely, the human affirmation of God's revelation and redemption in Christ. Yet for Barth the concept of experience is too loaded to be useful. 'The term is burdened – that is why we avoid it – with the underlying idea that man generally is capable of religious experience or that this capability has the critical significance of a norm' (*CD* I/1 193). The only norm is the wholly self-revealing Word of God. Both experience and faith, faith being for Barth a much more positive term than experience, are the result of and not the precondition for the acceptance of God's redemptive Word.

Barth, as we have seen, has already been thinking in threefold terms. 'In fact we can substitute for revelation, Scripture and proclamation the names of the divine persons Father, Son and Holy Spirit and *vice versa*' (*CD* I/1 121). The one God exists in three interdwelling persons, the *perichoresis* or mutual inter-relatedness of Father, Son and Spirit. Now he explains this in depth: 'God the Revealer is identical with his act in revelation and also identical with its effect' (*CD* I/1 296). In other words, the very concept of God's immediate self-revelation and human-kind's direct, immediate acceptance of it demands a doctrine of the Trinity. For Barth, it had become blindingly self-evident that God *himself* is the content of his revelation and not just facts about him, that God reveals himself *through* himself, and it is *God* who does the revealing. God is the revealer, God is the content of his self-revelation, and it is through God and in God that we are permitted to appropriate that reality for ourselves. This not only coincides with the New Testament witness to God as Father, Son and Holy Spirit but is demanded by the very logic of a sound theology: 'The God who reveals himself in the Bible must also be known in his revealing and his being revealed if it is he who is to be known' (*CD* I/1 298). Revelation, he repeats, 'is in every way identical with God himself' (*CD* I/1 299).

Revelation and Trinity

'In putting the doctrine of the Trinity at the head of all dogmatics we are adopting a very isolated position from the standpoint of dogmatic history' (*CD* I/1 300). The tendency in Western thought since the days of Augustine had been to treat the Trinity in an abstract fashion, a quasi-mathematical conundrum of three-in-one and one-in-three. By the post-Reformation period it had been more or less dispensed with as dry speculation. Even Protestant and Catholic orthodoxy neglected to give it pride of place: God's unity was centre stage; his tri-unity was derivative of the fact. What Barth did was to make God's tri-unity absolutely essential to the concept of revelation, and in so doing restore the Trinity to the mainstream of twentieth-century Christianity. According to John Webster, 'Barth rescued the doctrine of the Trinity from the obscurity in which it had languished in modern Protestant dogmatics.'[1]

'In God's revelation God's Word is identical with God himself' (*CD* I/1 304). This sums up Barth's statement 'that God reveals himself as the Lord' (*CD* I/1 306). This, for Barth, is 'the root of the doctrine of the Trinity', just as the Trinity is essential not only to how we can understand God and benefit from knowing him, but as to who God is in himself. For Barth, the eternal God possessed simplicity and a profound unity, but there was a differentiation within the deity that could not be denied. 'The God who has revealed himself according to the witness of Scripture is the same in unimpaired unity and yet also the same thrice in different ways in unimpaired distinction' (*CD* I/1 307). The one God exists in the unity of his essence as Father, Son and Holy Spirit, yet in distinctiveness as delineated by the three separate persons. The unity does not threaten the distinction nor does the distinction threaten the unity. This is as true for God's revelation, manifested to human beings as the 'economic' trinity, as it is for God's essence or eternal substance, namely his 'immanent' trinity. For Barth, the immanent, or essential, trinity is antecedent to the economic trinity, in other words, God is first in essence Father, *Logos* or divine Word, and Holy Spirit before revealing himself to humankind as such. But the revelation is a revelation of *God*: 'If we are dealing with his revelation, we are dealing with God himself and not, as modalists in all ages have thought, with an entity distinct from him' (*CD* I/1 311). Consequently, 'we arrive at the doctrine of the Trinity by no other way than that of an analysis of the concept of revelation' (*CD* I/1 312).

Although Barth preferred to call Father, Son and Holy Spirit the three 'modes' of the Trinity rather than three 'persons', he did this not because he was a modalist (as we have seen) or a Sabellian (that is, someone who believed that the one God only *appeared* in three separate forms but behind the forms was only one undifferentiated eternal being), but because the word 'person' had by the modern period lost its original signification and come to mean more or less an 'individual'. The biblical God was not three different individuals, rather God was the one God possessing three separate modes or states of being: 'We are speaking not of three divine "I"s, but thrice of the one divine "I"' (*CD* I/1 351). According to the Church's doctrine, there was, in fact, 'a distinction ... or order ... in the essence of God' (*CD* I/1 355). The three so-called 'I's were not simple repetitions of one another; they partook of specific functions, the Father as Creator or fountainhead of the deity, the Son reciprocating perpetually the Father's love in obedient response, and the Spirit freeing human beings to respond to the redemptive love that the Son had displayed (and made incarnate) in bearing the sin of humankind. (Each mode, or person, and its characteristics and role would be described in detail in *CD* I/1, §§ 10–12.) The three modes were, in fact, profoundly personal and mutually interactive.

Working with such unfamiliar conceptual tools as these, Barth was highly conscious of the novelty (and for many the sad anachronism) of his venture: 'Only pious reverence for a venerable landmark of Christianity has preserved some place for the Trinity ... in the Evangelical Church as it is now ravaged by modernism' (*CD* I/1 379). Yet what this preparatory assessment of the Trinity had achieved was not just to lay out the ground plan of Barth's whole structure on which the remaining four volumes of the *Church Dogmatics* would be so massively built, but to restore to the Protestant Church its theological soul.

If Barth's preliminary account of the Trinity constituted the first part ('The triune God') of chapter 2 in *Church Dogmatics* I/1, Part 2 of that chapter ('The incarnation of the Word of God') ran well into *CD* I/2, with his assessment of 'the Word, or God's objective revelation to humankind' (§§ 13–15), followed by Part 3, 'The outpouring of the Holy Spirit' (§§ 16–18), the subjective appropriation of that revelation by the believer and the community of faith.

Incarnation and freedom

God, in his sovereign liberty, is free to be humankind's God. There is nothing in God's deity or in the human nature of humankind to prevent God, were God so to desire, from becoming God for man. This, in fact, is what had occurred. It had occurred, though, not because it had to, or was destined to do so, but because God had chosen or elected for it to happen. Men and women have no hold on God. That Barth made this point at all was unprecedented, on this scale, in twentieth-century theology. Modern Protestantism had taken man's place in the scheme for granted, presupposing that it all existed for his salvation and hinged on him. Barth, however, challenged this presupposition absolutely, and begins with the sovereign freedom of God. It was certainly true that God had chosen for humankind, but God had done so as an act of sheer gratuity. We know this quite simply because of the concrete reality of Jesus Christ. Although fully human, Christ cannot be explained according to the already understood categories of ordinary humanity. He is not merely a religious prophet, a moral teacher, an example of all that is best in human nature and therefore, as liberal theology has posited, divine. Christ is unprecedented, the unique *Logos* of God who had made himself one with humankind.

> The answer of the New Testament to our question about the reality of God's revelation is to be found in the constant reiteration in all of its pages of the name Jesus Christ ... Jesus Christ is not one element in the New Testament witness alongside of others, but as it were the mathematical point towards which all the elements of the New Testament witness are directed. (*CD* I/2 10–11)

For Barth, all general religious and theological concepts must yield to the exclusive particularity of Jesus Christ. This is a basic motif in his whole scheme: 'Barth's theology makes a concerted attempt always to move from the particular to the general rather than from the general to the particular.'[2] Particularity begins with God's self-revelation in Jesus Christ.

Having made the point that Christ is the objective reality of revelation, he proceeds to show how this actually occurred. Drawing from the New Testament writers, he pictures the way the evangelists and St Paul described Christ's incarnate presence within the world: 'He became a real, genuine, true man, man placed before God' (*CD* I/2 40). Likewise, what was true of the particularity of Christ's *Incarnation* was true of the particularity of Christ's *time*. For Barth, it was a characteristic of modernity that people could only think in terms of mundane temporality, or history as a general truth. Christianity was expected to fit into a conceptual world that already existed and was thought to be self-evident and axiomatically true. It was no wonder, therefore, that the Incarnation became problematic and the resurrection explained ahistorically in terms of myth. Challenging the axioms of modernity head on, he asks what reality means. Is reality a given, independent of God, Christ and faith, or is a neutral, objective reality in fact a fiction and itself a myth? In terms of revelation, God is the Creator, Lord and redeemer of time, and in Christ had *made* time for us: 'The time God has for us is just this time of his revelation, the time that is real in his revelation, revelation time' (*CD* I/2 45). This too was an alien discourse in the context of current theology, and a wholly unfamiliar mode of reasoning that Barth was, with increasing confidence, making his own.

It was with § 15, 'The mystery of revelation', however, that Barth displayed a brilliance that put him into a category of his own. This paragraph, and the one following, 'The freedom of man for God', has been called 'the first truly great piece of writing in the *Church Dogmatics*, attaining a level of sustained conceptual and rhetorical grandeur equal to anything else Barth wrote.'[3] Essentially a treatise on Christology, 'If dogmatics cannot regard itself . . . as fundamentally Christology, it has assuredly succumbed to some alien sway' (*CD* I/2 123), it paves the way for the unprecedentedly rich, textured and multi-layered treatment of a Christ-centred reconciliation that would be pursued in *Church Dogmatics* IV. Revelation is the mystery of God having become human: 'Emmanuel, God with us', which Barth takes from the reference in Matthew's Gospel to the birth of Christ (Matthew 1.23), 'and the Word became flesh', which he takes from the prologue to the Gospel of John (John 1.14). The sign of this mystery is the miracle of the virgin birth. Here

Barth flies in the face of a scholarly consensus that, since the Enlightenment, had been perplexed by, embarrassed with or contemptuous of the claim that Christ had been conceived by the Holy Spirit. Christ's unique humanity, that he was *vere homo*, 'true man', was mediated through Mary, his mother, who provided all that was required for him to become one with humankind. Yet his miraculous conception through the Holy Spirit and not by Joseph signified that God had done a *new* thing. There was discontinuity, not continuity, between God's act in Christ and all other human phenomena. 'Human nature possesses no capacity for becoming the human nature of Christ,' he wrote. 'The virginity of Mary in the birth of the Lord is the denial . . . of any power, attribute or capacity in humankind for God' (*CD* I/2 188). This may indeed imply 'the proclamation of pure enigma' (*CD* I/2 185), but it was none the worse for that. It pointed, in fact, to the profound but exquisite mystery of the Incarnation of the Word, its boundary signs being the virgin birth on the one side and the empty tomb on the other.

As for humankind's freedom for God (the opening paragraph of Barth's treatment of the subjective aspect of God's self-revelation), under the guise of both liberalism and an uncritical pietistic orthodoxy, revelation had shaded off into the religious subject's inherent ability to take divinity into him or herself. Once more Barth blocks off this road unceremoniously. On the one hand, a free, unfettered human response is implied in God's sovereign call to people to affirm and believe the gospel. Human freedom is reflective of the sovereign freedom of God. The stock criticism of Barth, that he so magnifies God's sovereignty as to leave no room for human responsibility, is wholly misplaced: 'Not God alone, but God and man together constitute the content of the Word of God' (*CD* I/2 207). Yet, on the other hand, this freedom is not an autonomous facility of the human will, but partakes of the dynamic in which God has graciously elected to be one with humankind.

Barth would elaborate on the theme of human freedom significantly in his treatment of election in *Church Dogmatics* II, and the covenant in *Church Dogmatics* III. The basic conviction, however, is there from the beginning. Humankind is unfettered and free. Human beings' freedom is not some sort of objectivized ethical independence or psychological openness to the possibility of life, but the fruit of God's own gracious act through which Christ was elected as, and proclaimed himself to be, the covenant partner of all humankind. Philosophical debates about the freedom or bondage of the will are beside the point. And just as men and women are truly free, they are bidden joyously to live 'the life of the children of God' (§ 18).

The concept of Scripture

The two final chapters in *Church Dogmatics* I/2 involve Barth in a return to the threefold form of the Word of God, more especially to the doctrine of Scripture (chapter 3, 'Holy Scripture', §§ 19–21), and to a concluding assessment (yet again) of the nature of dogmatics (chapter 4, 'The proclamation of the Church', §§ 22–4). Both show how Barth's method functions. It is cyclical rather than linear, rhetorically complex and purposely repetitive. To understand Barth one needs to spend leisurely time with the *Church Dogmatics* – how he actually managed to write so extensively in such short periods between each successive volume is astonishing – to learn to be comfortable with his wholly counterintuitive technique, to allow him to dictate the pace and to put to one side most of the conventions of academic theology as they had been perfected since the Enlightenment. For the sake of brevity we shall only consider his treatment of the function of Holy Scripture within the Church.

The Bible, as we have already learned, is 'a witness to divine revelation' (*CD* I/2 457). As witness it is different from revelation, but as witness it is in faithful accord with that revelation and is the vehicle through which God actually and in reality reveals himself. Revelation is made manifest through the enscripturated words of the prophets and apostles. Theirs is 'human speech uttered by specific men at specific times in a specific situation, in a specific language and with a specific intention' (*CD* I/2 464). It never bypasses the human in some docetic fashion, and it will ever show itself to be the product of a human situation, though one in which God too was involved. Its purpose as Scripture is to manifest God's revelation of himself, yet that revelation is never a matter of words alone. What it does is to draw its hearers, or readers if the Bible is read, into a relationship with itself. Barth is not interested in a cool, neutral, unconcerned hermeneutic, but one in which the reader or listener displays an attitude of obedience and faith. In order to comprehend aright, the reader needs to be governed by the substance of God's active revelation in the words. We are, in fact, 'really to be open and ready, really to give ourselves to it', and by so doing, 'this mystery will create in us a peculiar fear and reserve which is not at all usual to us' (*CD* I/2 470). Although apparently subjectivist, Barth's thrust is quite the opposite from subjectivism. In his revelation, God allows himself to be objectively real to us and does so in the concrete reality that is the Holy Spirit.

As such, Scripture is self-authenticating: 'Scripture is recognized as the Word of God by the fact that it *is* the Word of God' (*CD* I/2 537, emphasis added). There are no criteria, extraneous to the fact of God's gracious and saving revelation of himself in the Word, by which we can prove this to be the case. Rather faith itself, bound to the Word and using the evidence of Scripture, attests to its nature as divine revelation. It was through the internal witness of the Holy Spirit and not so much any neutral process of logical deduction that the Church accepted the contents of the two testaments as God's unique Word: 'Scripture is holy and the Word of God because by the Holy Spirit it became and will become to the Church a witness to the divine event' (*CD* I/2 535). The canonical Scriptures of the Church derived their authority from the fact that they witnessed to the God who had been made manifest in Jesus of Nazareth who was Christ the Lord.

As we have seen, for Barth this was not an exercise in arbitrary believism but was demanded by the very logic of the theological discourse.

> Believing is not something arbitrary. It does not control its object. It is a recognizing, knowing, hearing, perceiving, thinking, speaking and doing which is mastered by its object. Belief that the Bible is the Word of God presupposes therefore, that this mastering has already taken place, that the Bible has already proved itself to be the Word of God, so that we can and must recognize it as such.
>
> (*CD* I/2 506)

His discovery of Anselm of Canterbury and his *credo ut intelligam* ('I believe so that I can understand') had affirmed Barth's insight that he here brought to bear on the doctrine of Scripture. God, being God, is beyond human rationality. In order to be known at all it is God who must disclose himself. Human rationality, freely acting in response to God's constantly disclosing act in the Holy Spirit, exists in order to confirm that disclosure once it has been made. There is no objectivity beyond that revealed by God.

How, therefore, should the authority of the Bible be understood? Protestant Biblicism had often resorted to 2 Timothy 3.16, 'All scripture is inspired by God', and 2 Peter 1.21, 'No prophecy ever came by human will, but men and women moved by the Holy Spirit spoke from God', in order to prove Scripture's infallibility. Such a stratagem had arisen from a concept of natural theology in which God's dynamic action in revealing *himself* had been eclipsed by a static notion of a God who could be proved by rational means. In order to defend the notion of divinity, the actual process whereby God had used flawed humankind to witness faithfully (and, in fact, infallibly) to himself had been abandoned. 'The Bible is not a book of oracles,' claimed Barth. 'It is genuine witness ... And how can it be witness ... if the actual purpose, act and decision of God in his only-begotten Son ... is dissolved ... into a sum total of truths abstracted from that decision?' (*CD* I/2 507). It is only by the miracle of divine revelation, and not by the use of a human philosophy of truth, that the link between God, the scriptural authors and ourselves can be made:

> The men whom we hear as witnesses speak as fallible, erring men like ourselves. What they say, and what we read as their word, can of itself lay claim to be the Word of God, but never sustain that claim ... The *theopneustia* (God-breathed character or inspiration) of the Bible, the attitude of obedience in which it was written ... is not simply before us because the Bible is before us and we read the Bible. The *theopneustia* is the act of revelation in which the prophets and apostles in their humanity became what they were, and in which alone in their humanity they can become to us what they are.   (*CD* I/2 507–8)

There is a mystery here beyond which we cannot proceed. Just as Christ was conceived of the Holy Spirit, and just as Christ is redemptively present in the Lord's Supper through the Holy Spirit, in the phenomenon of the Bible the miracle of his presence perpetuates itself: 'When we say "by the Holy Spirit" we say that in the doctrine of Holy Scripture we are content to give the glory to God and not to ourselves' (*CD* I/2 537).

6

The doctrine of God

The knowledge of God

How do we know God? And who is the God who can be known? As Europe was once more tearing itself apart, Karl Barth was asking these questions not as some intellectual speculation or idle game but in order to remind the Church that it had its own specific task to perform. Were these questions to be answered correctly, the Church would be strengthened in its mission to serve humankind, which had been elected in Christ to be God's own covenant partner and friend.

'In the doctrine of God we have to learn what we are saying when we say "God"' (*CD* II/1 3). In chapter 5 (§§ 25–7), 'The knowledge of God', Barth begins by claiming that, in fact, God is objectively known only to himself, but makes himself known mediately, not immediately, to humankind. God, of course, is *God*: 'God becomes, is and remains to [humankind] Another, One who is distinct from himself, One who meets him' (*CD* II/1 9). There is no blurring of the distinction between the Creator and the creature, and it is God who makes himself known. There is nothing on man's side that would favour such a move. Even when revelation occurs, it does so in a veiled fashion, through Scripture, proclamation and even through the human nature of Christ: 'Man cannot see God's face, God's naked objectivity, without exposing himself to the annihilating wrath of God. It would indeed have to be a second God who could see God directly. How could man escape destruction by God?' (*CD* II/1 19). Within the mysterious fellowship of the

Trinity, God does interact directly, God with God, but as for the rest of us, a veiling must occur: 'The Word of God does not appear in his eternal objectivity as the Son who dwells in the bosom of the Father. No, the Word became flesh' (*CD* II/1 19). We know God mediately or sacramentally, and the sacrament – a created reality through which the uncreated God gives himself to be known – is Jesus, Mary's son. What Barth is striving to say is that God ever preserves his primary object-ivity, though allowing himself to be known in a secondary objectivity, namely, in Christ. The knowledge of God is God's to give and not something that can be manipulated or controlled by anyone else. In other words, it is given to us as an act of grace and can only be known by faith.

In discussing 'The knowability of God' (§ 26), Barth returns to his dispute with both the Catholic dogma of the *analogia entis*, an innate source of divine knowledge independent of revelation ('I [still] regard the *analogia entis* as "the invention of anti-Christ"' (*CD* II/1 82)), and the sort of Protestant natural theology he had opposed in Brunner's work a few years earlier. The polemic is less heated and the discussion more nuanced, but no less real. Barth's complaint, invective apart, was not against people's capacity to know God but against believing that this capacity could be created or activated independently of God's unique revelation in Christ. God could be known not by any natural means but simply through Christ: 'If grace is alongside nature, however high above it it may be put, it is obviously no longer the grace of God but the grace which man ascribes to himself' (*CD* II/1 139). In becoming flesh, Jesus Christ has taken upon himself man's alienation from God, the judgement of God and his holy wrath, the accusation, condemnation and punishment of humankind, and through his sacrifice triumphed over alienation and sin: 'This victory of grace, this revelation of a truth and life of a new man, is called Jesus Christ' (*CD* II/1 153). What was revolutionary was Barth's marshalling of the evangelical categories usually connected with a doctrine of atonement to the assistance of an epistemology, or theory of knowledge, in which Christ himself, and not the cognitive abilities of the subjective individual, became essential in the process of knowing God. Natural theology, therefore, is ruled simply out of bounds. In fact, says Barth, 'it must be excised without mercy' (*CD* II/1 170).

In treating 'The limits of the knowledge of God' (§ 27), Barth retraces his steps, re-emphasizes the veiled, partial or hidden nature of God even in the process of his being revealed: 'The moment we have unreservedly to confess God's hiddenness, we have begun really and certainly to know God' (*CD* II/1 192). He is, however, insistent that this is not a matter of scepticism or the affirmation of a natural human inability to comprehend the divine, but paradoxically is God's way of truly *revealing* himself. God *reveals* himself to be hidden because God is God. Yet in Christ, this revelation makes itself available to humankind.

> In his revelation, in Jesus Christ, the hidden God has made himself apprehensible. Not directly but indirectly. Not to sight but to faith. Not in his being but in sign. Not, then, by the dissolution of his hiddenness – but apprehensibly . . . [for] the Word was made flesh.
>
> (*CD* II/1 199)

God is objective only to himself, but in Christ God equally objectively, but now in a mediate and not immediate form, becomes one with humankind. The hidden God can, therefore, be known, preached and thought about. Theology is yet possible. There is no reason for silence.

The reality of God

Having concluded chapter 5, 'The knowledge of God', Barth discusses, as every theologian must, 'The reality of God', the title of chapter 6 (§§ 28–31). That reality for Barth is active, dynamic, self-contained and uniquely particular. As has become evident, Barth never begins where virtually all modern Western theology had begun, namely, with general concepts of ontology and on that basis speculation as to who God was. Rather he begins with the particular reality witnessed to in Scripture, which found its focus and fullness in Jesus Christ. As such, God is 'the One who loves in freedom' (*CD* II/1 257). For Barth, the language of essence or being is static, impersonal, and gives itself too readily to be conceptually manipulated by theologians and believers alike. The biblical God, however, is Lord; God cannot be manipulated as God is eternal act: 'To its very deepest depths God's Godhead consists in the fact that it is an *event*' (*CD* II/1 263, emphasis added). The language of 'essence' or 'being' may legitimately be used, but only after having been commandeered by the fact that God in the very depths of his being is pure act: 'God exists in his act. God is his own decision. God lives from and by himself' (*CD* II/1 272).

This rather technical phraseology presupposes what Barth had already treated at length in *Church Dogmatics* I, that God exists actively as Father, Son and Holy Spirit. As the eternal fount of the deity, God acts in the eternal generation of the Son. The Son, as the eternal *Logos*, is perpetually responsive to the call of the Father, while the Spirit proceeds eternally from the Father and the Son. The language of classic trinitarianism points to an active reality within God's very essence that became known in the Incarnation of Christ, for which the biblical narrative, Old Testament as well as New, serves as a context. And, of course, love is at its very heart. It is the fact of revelation, and not any preconceived idea we may have had, that tells us God not only loves, but that God loves *us*. 'God is he who, without having to do so, seeks and creates fellowship between himself and us' (*CD* II/1 273). God's love is not a commonplace nor a cliché nor, for us at least, in any way inevitable. Rather it is sheer miracle, yet it is in accord with the active love that flows within the reality of the triune God.

The idea that Barth's doctrine of God is a tentative or theoretical exercise with no intrinsic bearing on humankind, although still popular in some quarters, is wholly erroneous. God's *being* is such that God chooses to love in freedom. Within the depths of the divine being, God chose to become one with humankind in Christ. Christ is not merely the Lord of the Church, or indeed a saviour for the religiously inclined, but, as the second Adam, the one in whom the whole of humankind is included. There is in all of Barth's work a profound and affirming humanism in which God, although sovereign, mighty and Lord, is never oppressive but provides the basis for a wholly unconstrained human flourishing. The rest (§§ 29–31) of chapter 6 is taken up with another highly original and in parts quite brilliant assessment of the attributes of God, what Barth prefers to call God's 'perfections' ('one of the finest accounts of the topic to be found in theological history'[1]), after which he proceeds to discuss the election of humankind in Christ. It is possible here only to list these perfections: the three paired perfections of love (grace and holiness, mercy and righteousness, patience and wisdom), and the three paired perfections of freedom (unity and omnipresence, constancy and omnipotence, wisdom and glory). Because all these perfections are grounded in Jesus Christ and not in some speculative divine principle, both love and freedom constitute the very essence of God's eternal being.

The doctrine of election

In turning to chapter 7 (comprising §§ 32–5) of *Church Dogmatics*, 'The election of God', which is the opening chapter of II/2 (published 1942), we come to another epoch-making portion of the theologian's work: 'When the history of the theology of the twentieth century is written . . . I am confident that the greatest contribution of Karl Barth to the development of church doctrine will be located in the doctrine of election.'[2] As a Reformed theologian, Barth was both drawn to the concept of election while very conscious of the difficulties the traditional doctrine posed. Yet he had formulated his basic principles which, as it happened, were wholly compatible with a notion of election, as long as it were defined wholly in terms of Jesus Christ. The insight he had gained via his friend Pierre Maury at the Calvin Conference in Geneva in 1936 had already given him pause to think: 'His address at once made a profound impression on me . . . One can certainly say that it was he who contributed decisively to giving my thoughts at this point their fundamental direction.'[3] Barth had shared his preliminary reflections with the audience of his Gifford Lectures in Aberdeen a year later. Now he expressed them fully, with immense creativity and poise.

Despite drawing much from Augustine and Calvin, Barth found himself having to cast the doctrine in a radically new mould: 'As I let the Bible itself speak to me on these matters, as I meditated on what I seemed to hear, I was driven irresistibly to reconstruction' (*CD* II/2 x). With Christ not only as the mirror of human election (as Calvin had so aptly claimed) but also its basis, means and content as well, there was no reason why the doctrine could not be positively affirmed: 'The election of grace is the sum of the gospel . . . The election of grace is wholly the gospel . . . It is the very essence of all the good news' (*CD* II/2 13–14). This was hardly the way the teaching had been perceived in the past, when it had been linked with notions of determinism, fatalism and an arbitrary decree whereby God had chosen some to be saved and allowed the rest to be damned. Having pondered Scripture afresh, not least the Old Testament conviction concerning Israel's election as a light to the nations and St Paul's mighty reasoning in Romans, he became convinced that the duality of election and reprobation, when severed from the all-embracing nature of Christ's atoning sacrifice, could not be sustained: 'In the Holy

Scripture there is no parallelism of this kind in the treatment and proclamation of the divine election and rejection' (*CD* II/2 16). The traditional supposition was that the Father, in issuing the redemptive decree, had done so with a view that the Son would become the saviour of the world. The function of the Son was responsive to the Father rather than having shared in the eternal accord. Yet Christ is the one in whom all things eternally occur: 'As we have to do with Jesus Christ, we have to do with the electing God' (*CD* II/2 54). Christ is not the one who merely responds to the Father's choice but is active in making that choice from the beginning. And as Christ becomes one with all of humanity, humanity lies within the scope of God's sovereign mercy, love and grace from the start. 'Election is that which takes place at the very centre of the divine Word' (*CD* II/2 59). It is Christ, therefore, sharing fully and actively in the Father's will, who 'is the electing God' (*CD* II/2 77).

The contentious implications of the older Calvinistic view had long been known. If God had elected only some to life, how could individuals know they were among the elect? Whereas John Calvin's pastoral sensitivity, as well as his theological acumen, had prompted him to devise the concept of Christ being the mirror of our election, this was not enough. It did not remove the possibility of there being a decree that somehow bypassed Jesus Christ and in which he as saviour was not involved. Even Calvin had spoken of the *decretum absolutum* ('absolute decree') as a *decretum horribile* ('dreadful decree'): 'If Jesus Christ is only elected and not primarily the elector, what shall we really know at all . . . of our election?' (*CD* II/2 104). The assurance of salvation, such a vexing problem in the Reformed tradition, had therefore found a solution: 'As we believe in him and hear his Word and hold fast by his decision, we can know with a certainty which nothing can ever shake that we are the elect of God' (*CD* II/2 116).

The electing God and the elect man

The concept of Christ being the electing *God* was, however, only half of the doctrine. In the Incarnation, the *Logos* of God had also become *man*. Nothing illustrates better Barth's startling originality of thought within the bounds of otherwise highly traditional orthodoxy than the assertion that God the elector, namely, Christ, elects *himself*, but this time as humankind's representative and substitute, and in so doing bears the wrath, judgement and damnation humankind has brought on itself: 'The election of the man Jesus means . . . that a wrath is kindled, a sentence pronounced and finally executed, a rejection actualized' (*CD* II/2 122). Double predestination in the older Calvinistic parlance was the belief that God had chosen some to be saved and others to be damned. It was a notorious doctrine that created endless controversy and strife. Rather than rejecting the concept outright Barth revolutionizes it, not by downplaying the notion of sin, judgement and righteousness but by centring it wholly on Christ. Damnation remains a fact, but it has been dealt with on the cross.

> The rejection which all men incurred, the wrath of God under which all men lie, the death which all men must die, God in his love for men transfers from all eternity to him in whom he loves and elects them, and whom he elects at their head and in their place.   (*CD* II/2 123)

As well as being the electing God, Christ was also the elect man in whom the whole of humankind exists and finds its fulfilment. In the light of such a reconstruction, which constituted 'an absolutely astonishing overturning of the tradition',[4] it is little wonder Barth could consider the doctrine of election to be a matter not of disconcertment but of comfort, indeed the very essence of all the good news.

It left, however, many questions unanswered. In dealing with the election of the community in § 34, Barth treats, not unexpectedly, the history of Israel and the Church, while § 35, on the election of the individual, discusses the enigma of those who seem not to be converted or, through their impenitence or continued rebellion, would seemingly put themselves outside of God's reach. Famously, Barth refuses to espouse the doctrine of the *apocatastasis*, universalism or the ultimate restoration of all things. Damnation remains a possibility, despite Christ having taken the divine judgement for all people upon himself. It is, paradoxically, an impossible possibility, a 'caricature and perversion' (*CD* II/2 315), a 'satanic possibility' (*CD* II/2 316) whereby the individual may 'choose the possibility which God has excluded by his election' (*CD* II/2 316). Here, however, we are in the bounds of speculation. This is God's concern, not ours. The thrust of the gospel is plain: 'The decree of God is not obscure, but clear . . . This decree is Jesus Christ, and for this very reason it cannot be a *decretum absolutum*' (*CD* II/2 158). Our concern is to witness to the gospel and to share the knowledge of God, trusting in 'the solidarity of the elect and the rejected in the one Jesus Christ' (*CD* II/2 347).

Theological ethics

Recent Barth scholarship has been very keen to remind us that Barth, throughout his career, was committed to the ethical task. God's self-revelation in Christ was not just a gospel but a demand. As God had called the human race to a covenant relationship with himself, the only apposite response was gratitude and obedience under the Word. Yet unlike conventional Christian ethics, in which the individual applied the divine instructions, whether the Ten Commandments or the Sermon on the Mount or the ethical portions of St Paul's epistles, to him- or herself, for Barth, Christ had already spoken, thus revolutionizing the whole process. God has spoken definitively in Christ, and Christ, as obedient humankind, has responded perfectly to the command of God. The Word that God has spoken to humanity is not a naked Word but has come clothed in Christ's own obedience. Consequently, when addressed to the hearer, the Word is not a developed moral code waiting to be applied but a 'command' that frees him or her to respond intelligently in obedience and faith. Chapter 8, 'The command of God', the second and concluding chapter of *Church Dogmatics* II/2, spells this out in detail. The word 'command' in these rich and expansive paragraphs (§§ 36–9) does not mean a stifling order that must be slavishly obeyed, but the dynamic in which the divine action, already made concrete in Christ, is constantly both being renewed and calling forth a free obedient response, through which human flourishing and sanctification occurs.

By the end of *Church Dogmatics* II/2, Barth was still less than halfway through his magnum opus. The doctrines of revelation and God fully explored, he now moved on to creation. It was the summer of 1942 and Barth, now aged 56, realized that he still had much work to do.

7

The doctrine of creation

The war years

Alongside his work on *Church Dogmatics* II during the war years, Barth issued numerous short tracts in support of those countries engaged in the struggle against Hitler. *A Letter to Great Britain from Switzerland* (1941) was one of these, written at the request of the ecumenical leader J. H. Oldham and including a foreword by the Anglican theologian Alec Vidler. Barth was garnering intense hostility within his own country by criticizing Switzerland for still trading openly with Germany under the guise of political neutrality. On a personal level, tragedy struck the Barth family with the death of Matthias, their third son, in a climbing accident in 1941. Like his brothers Marcus and Christoph, he was a theological student training for the ministry of the Reformed Church. Yet Barth's productivity was hardly diminished by either public disdain or personal loss during these years, nor was his taste for theological controversy. This was illustrated by a lecture of May 1943 in which he issued a searing critique of the Church's doctrine of baptism. Baptism was not a uniquely sacramental act, he claimed, but a free human witness to God's act in redeeming humanity in Christ. As such, neither the idea of mediating grace nor of infant participation was justifiable. 'The baptismal teaching prevalent today in all the great Christian confessions – including the Reformed Church – has in it . . . not a mere chink but a hole,' he claimed. 'In the sphere of the New Testament one is not *brought* to baptism, one *comes* to baptism' (*Bap.* 42). This concept of baptism was of a piece with the rest of Barth's theology. God's grace was sovereign. The idea of mediating grace through a human rite allowed the Church to commandeer revelation rather than to witness to it as a matter of free obedience. What was really at stake in the millennia-old perpetuation of infant baptism was not theology as such, he stated, but the vested interests of state Churches within the old Christendom.

At this time two years of war still lay ahead. Already lecturing to his students on *Church Dogmatics* III, on the doctrine of creation, Barth, like everyone else, yearned for the fall of Nazism and a cessation to Europe's tragedy. Yet with the final surrender of Germany in May 1945, joy was tempered by realization of the appalling destruction and by the numbing revelations concerning the fate of Europe's Jews. Karl took the opportunity to return to Germany as soon as possible, and in late September 1945, in Frankfurt, he met Martin Niemöller, newly released following nine years in solitary confinement. Barth returned again in November, to Stuttgart this time, where he met with George Bell, the Anglican Bishop of Chichester and the Confessing Church's (see Chapter 4) staunchest British ally, and the young Methodist scholar E. Gordon Rupp. The leaders of the German Evangelical Church, including Niemöller, had just issued the 'Stuttgart Declaration', in which they had admitted their complicity in Germany's guilt for allowing Nazism to prevail: 'Those who saw the Nuremburg criminals, led by Goering, come one by one to the microphone to say "Not Guilty!", cannot but think of those others, most of whom had been in prison for the gospel, with their affirmation of "Guilty".'[1]

Barth's principal contribution to the renewal of a shattered Germany, however, came in 1946, with his ministry in Bonn. Having been relieved from his responsibilities in Basel for the summer, he spent the semester in the ruins of his old university, delivering a series of lectures on the Apostles' Creed. This would become *Dogmatics in Outline* (1947), 'one of the great books of [the] century', according to the ethicist Stanley Hauerwas: 'No one can read this book and think that Barth was just another "theologian".'[2] Interest was intense: the gospel was being shown to be the basis of a true humanism on which a devastated Europe could be rebuilt.

Church Dogmatics III/1, consisting of chapter 9, 'The work of creation', had appeared in 1945. *CD* III/2, consisting of Barth's famous chapter 10, 'The creature', on anthropology, followed in 1948. *CD* III/3, consisting of chapter 11, 'The Creator and his creature', on providence, 'nothingness' and the angels, came in 1950, and *CD* III/4, consisting of chapter 12, 'The command of God the Creator', on the ethics of creation, in 1951. As though this were not enough, Barth was heavily involved in ecumenical work, including preparation for the World Council of Churches, established in Amsterdam in 1948 with support for the Churches in eastern Europe, who now had to face a new state tyranny under Communism. He was also countering Rudolf Bultmann's programme of 'demythologizing' the New Testament in an attempt to make the gospel resonate with modern preconceptions, and Emil Brunner had returned to the fray with a carping criticism of Barth's insufficiently robust response to the evils of state Communism. A feel for Barth's concerns during these years can be found in the aptly titled *Against the Stream*, a compendium of his shorter works issued in 1954 by the Scottish theologian Ronald Gregor Smith. Due to the immense scope of *Church Dogmatics* III, discussion here must be highly selective. The remainder of this chapter will précis some representative themes.

Knowledge of the Creator

In *Church Dogmatics* III/1, consisting of chapter 9, 'The work of creation' (§§ 40–2), Barth lays out his understanding of how we can know God as Creator. This has nothing to do with an abstract God or a generalized concept of a first cause or

God-principle. Rather it has to do with affirming the fact that God has already been revealed as humanity's Creator through the person of Jesus Christ: 'I believe in God the Father Almighty, Creator of heaven and earth.' This, of course, 'is an appeal to faith' (*CD* III/1 11). It cannot, of necessity, be an autonomous logical deduction based on neutral or so-called 'scientific' evidence, but is inevitably based on God's self-revelation in the Word: 'The whole Bible speaks figuratively and prophetically of [God], in Jesus Christ, when it speaks of creation, the Creator and creation' (*CD* III/1 23). As for scientific hypotheses concerning the creation of the world, they are not ruled out: 'There is free scope for natural science beyond what theology describes as the work of the Creator' (*CD* III/1 x). Scientists must be allowed to make their own evidence-based suppositions as to how the world began, but revelation possesses a validity of its own. The Church's faith in the Creator-God is rooted in the unique revelation in Christ, who in turn reveals the reality of the Father as the one who calls the universe – what the Bible calls 'heaven and earth' – into being: 'In the sense of the biblical witness from Genesis to the Revelation of John, [these two terms] denote the sum of the reality which is distinct from God' (*CD* III/1 17).

Creation and covenant

The bulk of Barth's discussion in these paragraphs is taken up with an extended piece of exegesis on Genesis 1—2. The form of the creation narrative is 'saga', and it exists in order to facilitate God's choosing to call humanity into fellowship with himself: 'Creation sets the stage for the story of the covenant of grace' (*CD* III/1 44). Barth is insistent that 'saga' is not myth. If myth is a pictorial way of describing a timeless, ahistorical truth, 'saga . . . is an intuitive and poetic picture of a prehistoric reality of history which is enacted once and for all within the confines of time and space' (*CD* III/1 81). The form of the creation narrative is patently pictorial and not literalistic. However, it diverges radically from Canaanite myth in not symbolizing a timeless reality but pointing, however obliquely, to a real occurrence within God's creation. Barth has been criticized for improbable interpretation in these sections, what one theologian has called 'a dazzling display of exegetical pyrotechnics',[3] but there is little doubt that his extensive exegesis of Genesis 1, 'Creation as the external basis of the covenant', covering over 230 pages in § 41, contains much thought-provoking material whose main weakness is an overemphasis on humanity's place within the covenant, to the detriment of that of the rest of the created order. Genesis 2, 'Covenant as the internal basis of creation', discussed in a further 130 pages of § 41, reverses the order but underlines the main point, that God's work in creation finds its goal and purpose in calling humankind, instituted in Christ through whom it will be redeemed, into fellowship with him. (What is seriously lacking throughout *Church Dogmatics* III is an exegetical treatment of Christ as the *medium* of creation as portrayed in the prologue to John's Gospel, Colossians 1 and Hebrews 1, and a corresponding assessment of its theological significance.)

Barth's closing paragraph to chapter 9, § 42, is entitled 'The "yes" of God the Creator'. Although the 'theology of crisis' belonged to the past, even in 1945 many still thought that the essence of Barth's theology was 'in the negative, judging, irrevocable and implacable No which was pronounced over every righteousness of men'.[4] In fact Barth's reputation for having violently repudiated natural theology and his aggressive use of the word 'No!' in the controversy with Emil Brunner had masked a wholly positive core conviction that the Word of God had affirmed all that was good and wholesome in human life. The final paragraph returns forcefully to this point: 'Divine creation is divine benefit . . . God the Creator did not say No, nor Yes and No, but Yes to what he had created' (*CD* III/1 330). Echoing the Genesis repetition, 'And God saw that it was good' (e.g. Genesis

1.10), Barth expatiates on the idea of creation's actualization, or God actively allowing creation to flourish, and creation's justification, the declaration in Christ that despite the enigmatic tragedy of sin and evil, God's good creation is really good. The only possible response is gratitude and praise: 'It is our duty . . . to love and praise the created order because, as is made manifest in Jesus Christ, it is so mysteriously well-pleasing to God' (*CD* III/1 370).

'Chapter 10'

For all the texture and innovativeness of *Church Dogmatics* III/1, there occurs a step change between it and the following part-volume, Barth's celebrated 'chapter 10' ('The creature'), his treatment of humankind as creature that constitutes the whole of *Church Dogmatics* III/2. The intricacy and multi-layered quality of this work is exceptional – a sheer theological brilliance is sustained throughout. Barth finds himself in constant dialogue with the classical Christian tradition, stimulated by its findings, challenged by its insights, always probing, sometimes rejecting it in parts but supremely transforming its content by the application of his own assumptions concerning the way God had called humankind into fellowship with himself in Christ. The scene is set in § 43, 'Man as a problem of dogmatics'. Barth blithely confronts modern theology's postulate that an objective anthropology can be attained independently of God's revelation in Christ, while thereafter fitting Christ into the scheme in order to say something about humankind and God. On the contrary, the key to a sound understanding of humanity is not humanity itself but Jesus Christ, God become flesh: 'As the man Jesus is himself the revealing Word of God, he is the source of our knowledge of the nature of man as created by God' (*CD* III/2 41). To be genuinely Christian, anthropology must function in the light of Christology and not vice versa. Like the rest of creation, humanity exists in relation to the covenant. Only after God's Word has been spoken can humanity be known as it really exists, and then become a sphere for independent understanding and inquiry: 'The nature of the man Jesus alone is the key to the problem of human nature ... He alone is primarily and properly man' (*CD* III/2 43).

The architecture of *Church Dogmatics* III/2 is elaborate and deliberate: § 44, 'Man as the creature of God', is paralleled by § 45, 'Man ... as the covenant partner of God', while the various sub-sections in each, 'Jesus, man for God' and 'Jesus, man for others', for instance, echo one another in a quite intentional way. One feature of the work is Barth's expansive debate with Johann Gottlieb Fichte, the nineteenth-century Romantic philosopher, Karl Jaspers, the twentieth-century existentialist, and even Emil Brunner, in which he accepts gladly those aspects of their thought that shed light on the human condition but is resolute in refusing to allow theological judgements to be made according to the canons of an independent philosophical scheme. The only thing that can constitute a true anthropology is Christ, God's 'Yes' to creation and the unprecedented revelation of God's self. Jesus' obedience, openness and fellowship with the Father provide the basis on which humanity exists in obedience, openness and fellowship with God. Far from being exemplarist, this Christology (which is wholly in tune with Chalcedonian orthodoxy, namely, that Jesus is fully God and fully human) is constitutive of humankind's very being: 'His being as a man ... reveals and explains human nature with all its possibilities' (*CD* III/2 59). Although he makes heavy demands on his readers in these sections, there is a freshness and creativity in Barth's use of Christology as being constitutive of human existence that is consummately profound.

'The real man'

For Barth, human reality has been altered by the fact that Jesus Christ has assumed human nature, whether men and women are conscious of the fact or not. This is not a 'religious' affirmation but the essence of human existence as such. Because this is the case, man's true being consists of the fact 'that he is with Jesus and therefore with God' (*CD* III/2 135). The term Barth uses is 'derivation' – we derive our existence from Christ, the divine *Logos*, the elect of the Father, who has freely chosen to be humanity's representative, saviour and friend. Human existence is different from that of God. Divinity can never be predicated to man even though, in Christ, God has become man. God remains God even in Jesus Christ, the bearer of God's wholly transcendent otherness. But humanity, as constituted in Christ, is wholly separate, autonomous (in the correct sense) and free. Its autonomy, though, derives from God's free grace and finds its meaning and fulfilment in obedience, responsiveness and faith. The key to the concept of 'derivation' is the doctrine of election. In creating man as man, God has eternally decided for him, and in so doing affirmed his 'Yes' to creation, an affirmation that became manifest in the Incarnation and atoning sacrifice of Christ: 'To be a man is to be with Jesus . . . to be with the One who is the true and primary elect of God' (*CD* III/2 145). Christ is the effective enactment of the purpose through which human beings exist. Being elect means, in effect, being human. Both are the result of God's sovereign, all-embracing mercy in Christ. Election, therefore, can never stifle human receptivity, but rather set it free to fulfil its destiny and purpose.

Another way that Barth describes this 'derivation' is in terms of summons and call: 'Men are those who are summoned by the Word' (*CD* III/2 150). This call is not so much an overbearing or repressive command as an invitation to partake in that fellowship that is constitutive of humanity's very essence. Man is addressed, summoned and appropriated by the Word. This makes godlessness 'an ontological impossibility' (*CD* III/2 146). When it does occur, as undoubtedly it does, it does so as an enigma, a perversion and inexplicable reversion of God's elective will. The existence of sin, unbelief and evil, although real, are wholly paradoxical. Sin contradicts human existence, and though man may choose this impossibility, 'and grasping, he falls into the abyss' (*CD* III/2 147), sin can never imperil his true existence or call it into question in any way. Barth will expand on this in the extraordinary paragraph § 50, 'God and nothingness', in *Church Dogmatics* III/3. As for man's true existence, being elect in Christ, it is derivative of the divine call. The only valid response is gratitude, *eucharistia*, responding to *charis*, God's free though costly grace: 'Gratitude is the precise creaturely counterpart to the grace of God' (*CD* III/2 166). This too constitutes what it means to be truly human: 'Only as he thanks God does man fulfil his true being ... In this action alone is he man' (*CD* III/2 170–1). This is not a matter of attitude alone but of action: 'Human thanksgiving has the character of responsibility' (*CD* III/2 174). This, for Barth, is what it means to be 'the real man'.

That part of § 44 that deals with 'The real man' is only one portion of a rich and imaginative anthropology that weaves together such concepts as grace, obedience, Christology, the divine action, election and unfettered human response in an unprecedentedly varied way. The same level of insight and sophistication is found in the closing paragraphs, § 46, 'Man as soul and body' (95 pages) and § 47, 'Man in his time' (150 pages). Among the themes treated are the *imago Dei*, a social concept of humanity in which male and female reciprocity is deemed essential, the relation of the Holy Spirit to the created spirit of man, the physicality of the resurrection and the historicity of the Easter event (Barth's sparring partner here is Rudolf Bultmann and his programme of demythologizing the New Testament), along with much sobering but ultimately uplifting material on death and the final judgement. 'Barth enjoys himself in this volume as nowhere else in the *Church Dogmatics*: seriousness in approaching creation is not incompatible with delight in the subject matter.'[5] He certainly delights in treating these themes with intense mastery and at length. In all, chapter 10 is undoubtedly a tour de force.

God's providence

Chapter 11, 'The Creator and his creature', consisting of four long paragraphs (§§ 48–51) on providence, 'nothingness' and the angelic realm, constitute *Church Dogmatics* III/3, and chapter 12, 'The command of God the Creator', five intricate paragraphs on the ethics of creation (§§ 52–6), make up *Church Dogmatics* III/4. Like his doctrine of God, Barth's treatment of providence is both highly unusual and rooted soundly in tradition. It is also typical of all that we have now come to know concerning his method and style. For one thing, Barth's concern is 'to hold fast at all costs and at every point to the Christological thread' (*CD* III/3 xi). Consequently, it is non-speculative. He never speculates as to how God preserves, accompanies or rules over his creation, he merely keeps hold to the claim, made by and in Christ, that God is the loving Father whose Lordship is a fact. In other words, providence is a belief in God and his Lordship. It is not a means whereby the individual, as believer, or the Church, can track the way in which their own experiences or history have fitted into an elaborate or simple plan. Individuals may indeed do this, but providence exists apart from an ability to discern, or not discern, any pattern being worked out. It is, simply, a matter of faith: 'The Christian belief in providence is faith in the strict sense of the term' (*CD* III/3 15). The doctrine witnesses to God's paternal benevolence revealed in Christ, that God governs both heaven and earth, and that God is the Lord of history. The 'therefore' of faith, based on God's might, goodness and authority, witnessed not speculatively but in the Incarnation and resurrection of Christ, illuminates the 'nevertheless' of contradictory phenomena, and holds them in check. History, therefore, is not absurd and meaningless, but the '*theatrum gloriae Dei*' ('the theatre of God's glory'), however veiled it may be (*CD* III/3 48). The only key to true understanding is faith's sure knowledge of God; knowledge of the Ruler yields knowledge of the rule.

'God the Father as Lord of his creature', § 49, contains an assessment of the three customary aspects of providence, namely, *conservatio* (preservation), *concursus* (accompaniment) and *gubernatio* (governance or rule). In Christ, God preserves, sustains and upholds his creation, accompanies it and rules it for its own good and that of humanity, in the light of the eternal covenant secured in Christ. How this occurs is wholly a mystery. The speculative belief that God 'controls' all things in a mechanical or magical way, either coercing his creatures, impinging on their free choice, living their lives for them or overseeing their every move, is nowhere countenanced. There is no doubt that God is sovereign, but the perverse enigma of evil 'exists' while men and women are wholly free. It is within this dynamic that 'a motivative history' is created, a 'formative economy which assigns to all things a place, time and function' (*CD* III/3 192). This is not a matter of proof or logic, or a defence against tragedy, but an affirmation of God's elective revelation as the Father and Lord. The pattern is the Lord's Prayer taught by Christ himself and enacted by the elect man. We pray, 'our Father', asking that his will be done, while living our lives in free and functioning obedience. Divine will and human freedom may be logically incompatible, but the biblical revelation is quite oblivious to the fact. Logically it is a mystery, but theologically it is all of a piece: 'A high tolerance for mystery is a hallmark of Barth's theology – a tolerance which at once separates him from the standard modern theologies and unites him with the historical faith of the ecumenical church.'[6] That Barth concludes this paragraph not with an exercise in rational apologetics but with a meditation on prayer is wholly in accord with his whole scheme.

Nothingness, the angels and ethics

God's good creation is preserved from 'nothingness' (§ 50), namely, the baffling negative reality that was not created by God but nevertheless exists in opposition to God and his all-embracing, elective will. 'This menace' (*CD* III/3 296), which can never be relativized, synthesized, trivialized or domesticated, can only be encountered in the knowledge that it has been defeated by the ultimate victory of Jesus Christ:

> In the incarnation God exposed himself to nothingness even as this enemy and assailant. He did so in order to repel and defeat it. He did so in order to destroy the destroyer . . . He shows himself to be the total victor.
>
> (*CD* III/3 311)

Barth completes *Church Dogmatics* III/3 with the most extensive treatment of angelology since St Thomas Aquinas. Cocking a typical snook at the sophisticated modern mind, he reminds his readers that the Bible takes the angels seriously, and so should we: 'To deny the angels is to deny God himself' (*CD* III/3 486). They cannot be demythologized because, like the virgin birth, the New Testament miracles, the resurrection and the second coming, they belong to that realm that constitutes objective reality in which God has revealed himself. 'I do not claim to have understood all that Barth has written in this chapter', stated W. A. Whitehouse, but his doctrine of the angels 'worked out so magnificently [here] . . . is something vital to our apprehension of the gospel'.[7]

Church Dogmatics III/4, 'The command of God the Creator', like *Church Dogmatics* II/2, 'The command of God', has to do with ethics. The idea that Barth had no place for moral theology within his scheme is palpably untrue. In fact 'he insisted that ethics be treated not as an afterthought, but within the very fabric of dogmatics'.[8] Most books on theological ethics begin with a treatment of theory, whether deontology, natural law or whatever, move to Scripture and its application, and then treat specific issues. Barth, of course, circumvents this scheme by founding everything on revelation, election and the specific command of Christ. It is not that individual issues are ignored. There is much that is salutary in §§ 54–5 on sexual ethics, family relations, parental discipline, birth control, ethnicity and national identity, individual rights, animal rights, asceticism, health and sickness, abortion, capital punishment, warfare and recreation. Yet the reader will seek in vain for 'rules' that can be applied independently of an ever fresh and individual response to the specific command of Christ in each specific circumstance. Like manna, grace cannot be stored. Similarly, the ethical life cannot be lived according to disembodied 'rules', even those of Scripture, but by attending ever anew to what Christ has to reveal to those who live conscientiously in free obedience to him.

8

The doctrine of reconciliation

The 1950s

Barth began work on *Church Dogmatics* IV, *The Doctrine of Reconciliation*, in 1951. By now he was 65 years old. He hardly realized that *CD* IV would stretch to nearly 3,000 pages, over four volumes (in the English translation), with a fifth part-volume, on baptism, appearing in 1967, the year before he died. What was left, though still uncompleted, was issued posthumously. *Church Dogmatics* IV would be Barth's crowning masterpiece, 'one of the incontestably great pieces of Christian literature of the century',[1] which would consume him throughout the 1950s and sap his energy during the final decade of his life. It was more intricately designed and executed than its predecessors, and weaved together all his previous themes: revelation, the Trinity, election, Christology, faith, obedience and human freedom, in an exquisite if complex pattern. According to T. F. Torrance, '*CD* IV surely constitutes the most powerful work on the doctrine of atoning reconciliation ever written, in which Patristic and Reformation insights are interwoven into a single fabric.'[2] It defies abridgement, but will be the concern of the latter part of this chapter.

If the practical aftermath of the war had been one of Barth's major concerns during the later 1940s, the international situation was the backdrop to his theological labours throughout the following decade. Cold-war paranoia was affecting even neutral Switzerland, with a crescendo of opposition to Barth's refusal to demonize the communist East and his corresponding opposition to German militarization. He carried on doing theology as usual, and although he was secure in his status as the world's leading Protestant dogmatician, he was far from being universally appreciated. He was, though, still drawing students from around the world, including Britain and the United States, and in 1951 instituted a regular English-language colloquium to cater for their needs. The delightful *Karl Barth's Table Talk* (1963) gives a vivid insight into the liveliness of this seminar group.

Barth's seventieth birthday in May 1956 was an opportunity for both celebration and taking stock. Despite his having included humankind in his understanding of God's self-revelation even from the beginning, he still retained the reputation of disparaging humanity. In a widely reported lecture, 'The humanity of God', he laid this ghost to rest. There was no retraction at all of the early work:

> What began forcibly to press itself upon us about forty years ago was not so much the humanity of God as his *deity* – a God absolutely unique in his relation to man and the world, overpoweringly lofty and distant, strange, yes even 'wholly other'. (*HG* 33)

The pastor of Safenwil had been unflinching in his task: 'The ship was threatening to run aground; the moment was at hand to turn the rudder an angle of exactly 180 degrees' (*HG* 38). That having been done, in the Romans commentary and the polemics that followed, he could then afford to rethink how God related to his world and formulate a true humanism rooted in humankind's gracious election in Christ as God's covenant partner, companion and friend: 'It is a matter of *God's* sovereign togetherness with man, a togetherness grounded in him and determined, delimited and ordered through him alone' (*HG* 42). The lecture underlined, in an accessible fashion, the humanism that had been basic to the whole *Church Dogmatics* project,

and also served as a précis of parts of what Barth would have
to say in *CD* IV.

The final decade

By 1961 Barth had reached his seventy-fifth year. Although he
found work on the *Church Dogmatics* increasingly arduous,
he still had an amazing capacity for hard work, while his spirit
was as indomitable as ever. Due to a special dispensation, he
had not been required to quit his chair at the statuary age of
70, but his retirement had now become inevitable. Controversy
dogged even this occasion when the university authorities over-
ruled the faculty's decision on the appointment of a successor.
Barth had been keen to see Berlin's Helmut Gollwitzer taking
his place, but the celebrated German's radical politics counted
against him in Basel. Following a protracted dispute, Barth's
chair was filled by the young Swiss, Heinrich Ott.

Barth's swansong was a special series of lectures that recap-
itulated his basic themes. Delivered in Basel during the winter
of 1961–2, and again, in English, during a lively tour of the
United States the following spring, *Evangelical Theology: An
Introduction*, and its author, were given a rapturous welcome:
'With its efforts, evangelical theology responds to this gracious
Yes, to God's self-proclamation made in his friendliness towards
man. It is concerned with God as the God of *man*, but just for
this reason, also with man as *God's* man' (*ET* 17). Barth was
accompanied on the American trip by his sons Christoph,
an Old Testament specialist who had long been a missionary
teacher in Indonesia, and Marcus, by then a New Testament
professor in Chicago.

Bereft thereafter of the stimulation of regular teaching, work
on the *Church Dogmatics* nearly lapsed. Barth was dismayed at
the state of current theology: 'If only I had not been gripped
by a lassitude bordering on acedia in relation to the whole
theological scene,' he wrote to Gollwitzer following his return

from the United States (*L* 61). By now the 1960s, the decade of the secular, had begun, and a virulent reaction against the values of the previous generation had become apparent. In theology, the existentialism of Rudolph Bultmann and Paul Tillich had become the norm, and Dietrich Bonhoeffer's 'religionless Christianity', popularized by John Robinson, the Anglican Bishop of Woolwich, in his *Honest to God* (1963), became one of the fashionable concepts of the time. 'The work of the Bultmannians (I call them the company of Korah!)[3] . . . spreads like a stain on blotting paper,' Barth wrote, its effect being heightened by 'this awful *Honest to God* man from England' (*L* 109, 150).

> I am not angry with the Korahites because of their demythologizing but because they try to eliminate the subject, the person of God . . . so that the person of God evaporates and merges into faith, and we end by being asked to have faith in our faith. That is arrant nonsense.
>
> (*FGG* 90)

One beacon of light that Barth claimed to perceive was not within Protestantism at all but in the Second Vatican Council, convened by Pope John XXIII in 1961 and then presided over by Pope Paul VI. It was Roman Catholic scholars such as Hans Urs von Balthasar, Henri Boulliard and latterly Hans Küng who had shown some of the most perceptive understanding of Barth's project. In fact in 1963 he had been invited to become an observer at one of the Council's sessions but, because of ill health, had had to refuse. Though very frail, he did eventually accept the Pope's invitation to Rome late in 1966 to discuss matters of mutual theological interest.

By then Barth's health was in obvious decline. As it happened, his unstintingly loyal assistant, Charlotte von Kirschbaum, had been struck by a dementia-like disease at the same time, and had to be consigned to a care home. By now Barth and his wife Nelly had been totally reconciled, and they visited 'Lollo' faithfully, despite her inability any longer to recognize them. Barth's eightieth birthday celebrations in May 1966 were a joyous affair, attended by civic and church dignitaries as well as family and friends. In a characteristically humorous speech, he listed his debts and noted his achievements, at one point likening himself to the beast that carried Christ into Jerusalem:

> I just happened to be on the spot. A theology somewhat different from the current theology was apparently needed at the time, and I was permitted to be the donkey that carried this theology for part of the way, or tried to carry it as best I could. (*FGG* 117)

It was a theology that centred on Jesus Christ's sacrificial condescension in reconciling the world to himself, and it was in *Church Dogmatics* IV that it was most fully set out.

The Lord as servant: God's humility in Christ

The design of *Church Dogmatics* IV is striking, powerful, beautiful and unique. Never before had such varying salvific motifs been brought together in such harmony. In § 58, namely, the second paragraph of chapter 13 ('The subject-matter and problems of the doctrine of reconciliation'), which is the first of the two chapters contained in *CD* IV/1, published in 1953, Barth provided his readers with a survey of the doctrine of reconciliation to be developed in the rest of *CD* IV/1 and its two successors, IV/2 and IV/3 (1955 and 1959). Barth took from Calvin and the Reformed tradition the *munus triplex* – Christ's threefold work as prophet, priest and king – though he changed the order: IV/1, chapter 14, entitled 'Jesus Christ, the Lord as servant', which would cover Christ's priestly role; IV/2, comprising chapter 15 ('Jesus Christ, the servant as Lord'), covering his kingly work; and IV/3, comprising chapter 16 ('Jesus Christ, the true witness'), which treated Christ's office as prophet. The volumes would include five symmetrical paragraphs, each covering parallel aspects of the doctrine – see Table 1 overleaf.

Table 1 The structure of *Church Dogmatics* IV/1–IV/3

CD IV/1	CD IV/2	CD IV/3
Priestly office	Kingly office	Prophetic office
§ 59 Obedience	§ 64 Exaltation	§ 69 Witness
§ 60 Sin as pride	§ 65 Sin as sloth	§ 70 Sin as untruth
§ 61 Reconciliation as justification	§ 66 Reconciliation as sanctification	§ 71 Reconciliation as vocation
§ 62 Gathering of the Church	§ 67 Upbuilding of the Church	§ 72 Sending of the Church
§ 63 Holy Spirit and faith	§ 68 Holy Spirit and love	§ 73 Holy Spirit and hope

Commencing chapter 14 with § 59, 'The obedience of the Son of God', Barth considers three interconnected themes: Christ's coming among us as our divine and human saviour, 'The way of the Son into the far country'; his taking our sin upon himself and dying on the cross, 'The judge judged in our place'; and 'The verdict of the Father', namely, Christ's resurrection from the dead on the first Easter morning. If Rudolf Bultmann's popular theology devalued the narrative history of the New Testament in favour of an ahistorical encounter that vouchsafed authentic existence for the modern believer, Barth is completely at home in the New Testament world, replete with miracles, following Jesus first in his Galilean ministry, then into Jerusalem for the passion, and finally among the resurrection accounts in the gospel stories. The hermeneutical key throughout is Jesus' sublime humility in choosing to venture deep into alien territory – the land of human sinfulness – in order to reconcile a lost world to God: 'In being gracious to man in Jesus Christ, he also goes into that far country, into the evil society of this being which is not God and against God' (*CD* IV/1 158). Whereas traditional theology had linked the humanity of Christ with his state of humiliation, and his deity with his ascended glory, Barth reverses the order, in keeping with his activist doctrine of God. Deep in his Trinitarian being God chose to be for humankind, therefore it is Christ's *deity* that displays obedience: 'God is not proud. In his high majesty he is humble' (*CD* IV/1 159).

In treating Christ's sacrificial death on the cross, Barth takes human sinfulness, rebellion and antipathy to God in deadly earnest. Sin provokes the divine wrath and must be punished. Atonement is vicarious and substitutionary:

> The mystery of his mercy is also the mystery of his right-eousness. He did not take the unreconciled state of the world lightly, but in all seriousness. He did not will to overcome and remove it from without but from within.
>
> (*CD* IV/1 237)

His was not 'an act of arbitrary kindness' (*CD* IV/1 237) but a costly redemption in which Christ, as man's righteous judge, took it upon himself to be judged in his place, though the Father vindicated the Son by resurrecting him from the dead. Consequently, human history has been changed irrevocably. While Bultmann demythologized the resurrection, arguing that it belongs to an ahistorical realm, for Barth, it belongs to the realm of concrete historical fact: 'It has happened in the same sense as his crucifixion and his death, in the human sphere and human time, as an actual event within the world with an object-ive content' (*CD* IV/1 333). This was of a piece with Barth's understanding of the factual nature of God's dealing with his creation. Both cross and resurrection have had an altering effect on human reality as such:

> In virtue of the divine right established in the death of Jesus Christ, in virtue of the justification which has come to them in his resurrection, [men and women] are no longer what they were but they are already what they are to be ... They are no longer sinners, but righteous. They are no longer lost, but saved ... The resurrection of Jesus Christ

affirms that which is actual in his death, the conversion of all people to God which has taken place in him.

(*CD* IV/1 316–17)

Barth does not doubt that few are conscious of this fact or have responded to it in faith. Nevertheless, through the Father's powerful verdict on the sacrificial obedience of God the Son a new reality has dawned and human history has been changed forever.

Rather than beginning his doctrine of atonement with an account of humankind's need to be saved, true to his christological method Barth deals with sin in the context of Christ's costly obedience: 'Only when we know Jesus Christ do we really know that man is the man of sin and what sin is, and what it means for man' (*CD* IV/1 389). In the light of Christ's humility, sin is revealed as self-exaltation, and § 60 assesses sin in terms of pride. In the divine economy, pride is overcome through humility, which in turn is the basis of Jesus' righteousness in obedience to the Father's will. Consequently, justification, the theme of § 61, is based on the humility of Christ. Justification, which is accessed freely through faith, is always a mystery and a marvel: '[It] is always a strange righteousness: *iustitia aliens*, because first and essentially it is *iustitia Christi*' (*CD* IV/1 549). Through this mystery, sinners are pardoned and acquitted of their sins. In a sermon preached at the Basel prison around this time, Barth spoke of the stupendous wonder of salvation through grace by referring to an incident in Swiss folklore:

> You probably all know the legend of the rider who crossed the frozen Lake of Constance by night without knowing it. When he reached the opposite shore and was told whence he came, he broke down, horrified. This is the human situation when the sky opens and the earth is bright, when we may hear: *By grace you have been saved!* ... From this darkness he has saved us. He who is not

shattered after hearing this news may not yet have grasped
the Word of God: *By grace you have been saved.*

(*DC* 38)

The two final paragraphs of chapter 14, §§ 62–3, take the theme
of Christ's divine humility forward in terms of the communal
response to it, namely, the Church, and in terms of the faith of
the individual believer. Barth's treatment of the four 'notes' of
the Church – its unity, holiness, catholicity and apostolicity –
contains much on such subjects as 'nominal' in contrast to 'real'
Christians, the apostolic succession and the like, that is salutary
and wise, though the objectifying work of the Holy Spirit in
gathering the community through the Word is never threatened.
However important are the Church, and the individual's faith,
in the Christian scheme, their basis must always be Christ alone:
'The Jesus Christ attested in Scripture ... is single, unitary, con-
sistent and free from contradiction, yet ... his form is inex-
haustibly rich' (*CD* IV/1 763).

The servant as Lord: humankind's exaltation in Christ

The older Barth became the more prolix he tended to become,
not because of an innate verbosity but due to the expansive
nature of his subject matter. *Church Dogmatics* IV/2 (1955) is
well over 800 pages long, its five paragraphs being divided
into numerous sub-sections. If Christ's humble deity was
the theme of *CD* IV/1, the Saviour's exalted and victorious
humanity is expounded throughout *CD* IV/2: 'It was God
who went into the far country, and it is man who returns
home' (*CD* IV/2 21). The parallels are everywhere apparent.
The opening, § 64, includes sub-sections on 'The homecoming
of the Son of Man'; 'The royal man', dedicated to elucidating
Christ's kingly office; and 'The direction of the Son', which
explains how his resurrected humanity becomes the basis
for freedom and human activity in response to God's call.

Throughout this luxuriant paragraph, Christ is seen to act in free obedience to the Father's will and thus provide men and women, each of whom is in a covenant relation with God, with the means through which they can fulfil their human calling. Once again it is Christology, atonement, election, made active in 'the royal man', and not the moral or religious striving of the individual soul, that supply the basis for human flourishing and fulfilment.

If it is axiomatic in Barth that sin is revealed not through the preaching of an autonomous divine law or through psychological introspection, but simply through the presence of Christ – 'Where there is a genuine knowledge of sin, it is a matter of the Christian knowledge of God, of revelation and of faith, and therefore of the knowledge of Jesus Christ' (*CD* IV/2 381) – the form in which Christ's exaltation reveals sinfulness is that mediocrity, pettiness and trivial indifference that Barth, in a shrewd assessment in § 65, terms 'sloth'. There is nothing dramatic or Promethean in this self-indulgent indolence: it is 'merely banal and ugly and loathsome' (*CD* IV/2 404). This leads in turn (in § 66) to a detailed, and characteristically Reformed, discussion of holiness in which God, though retaining his sovereign freedom in the exalted Christ, calls men and women to partake in the freely willed and dynamic process of sanctification. What is striking throughout this treatment is the way the author draws his readers into the biblical world, the New Testament especially, by an incessant exegesis of Scripture. Barth's deep aversion to a speculative theology divorced from God's ongoing self-revelation, focused here in the risen Christ, is nowhere more pronounced.

In the final two paragraphs of *CD* IV/2, §§ 67–8, Barth returns to the concept of the Church and the individual believer, though the underlying theme this time is the Spirit's fruit of love. The Church, Christ's body constantly actualized in the Spirit and perceived by faith, is built up by sacrificial service and exists for the world. It is, in fact, 'a provisional representation of the

sanctification of all humanity . . . as it has taken place in [Christ]'
(*CD* IV/2 614).

The true witness

In his prophetic office Jesus Christ witnesses to the truth
he himself embodies: 'As he lives, Jesus Christ . . . is his own
authentic witness . . . He grounds and summons and creates
knowledge of himself and his life' (*CD* IV/3 46). That truth
encompasses both his priestly work in which, having chosen
to have fellowship with man, he has atoned for the sins of
the world and reconciled humankind with God (*CD* IV/1),
and his kingly role in which as the elect man, victorious and
resurrected, he has enacted a new reality that embraces all
people (*CD* IV/2). Christ, as God–man, bears effective witness
to this dual truth in such a way that it embeds itself within the
realm of human subjectivity. The reconciliation of humankind with God has been achieved. It needs nothing, from
our side, in order to be made effective. Although complete
in itself, it draws human beings into its orbit so that they can
participate in its reality while retaining their sovereign freedom
under the sovereign freedom of God. In other words, the
New Testament Christ is present, in however veiled a form, in
the essence of all things. He is the one in whom all things cohere
and through whom all things were made and have been
radically renewed. This, for Barth, is 'the glory of the mediator'
(§ 69), and it is through his prophetic office that this glory is
proclaimed.

The three parallel truths with which Barth begins *Church
Dogmatics* IV/3 (which at 930 pages had to be bound in two
tomes) are Jesus Christ as 'the light of life'; 'Jesus as victor', a
phrase he took from the charismatic ministry of J. C. Blumhardt,
the father of one of his Safenwil mentors; and 'the promise of
the Spirit'. Jesus is the one in whom God's inextinguishable
light shines, being reflected and refracted in all manner of

places and things. It is here that Barth discusses those 'other lights' (*CD* IV/3 97) and 'parables of the kingdom' (*CD* IV/3 114), namely, secular realities outside of the Church, with no formal link with the gospel but that nevertheless testify to God's redemptive truth. They exist quite simply because Christ is the truth. His light has enlightened all who have come into the world (John 1.9). Truth is where you find it, but it has been imparted by this one Christ. To assent to this is not to indulge in 'natural theology' or even to affirm a 'natural law' or 'natural revelation', it is merely to accept the way in which Christ's glory has manifested itself.

The content of this prophetic Word is one of victory, and Christ himself is the victor. The light shines in the darkness but darkness cannot overcome it. For Barth, this revelation of God's glory and the reconciliation achieved in Christ are one and the same: 'He himself is the revelation that he announces' (*CD* IV/3 183). There is nothing that human beings can do, even believing, obedient human beings, that can fulfil, complete or verify this reconciliation. Neither can it be vanquished or diminished in any way. That is not to say that it will not be challenged and resented: 'The meaninglessness and unfounded opposition of the world, the absurd fact of ignorance of himself' (*CD* IV/3 191) will persist. Such is 'the falsehood and condemnation of man' (§ 70), human sinfulness as it is revealed by the truth of Christ, God's witness. The thrust of the gospel, however, which includes the victory of the cross and God's stupendous act in the resurrection of Christ, shows that this radical contradiction is, in fact, doomed. It is the mission of the Holy Spirit which, in Johannine language, witnesses to Christ, to manifest this victory, and the Spirit does so by revealing the truth of the risen Christ: 'In the appearing of this man Jesus in the glory of God, the future, aim and end of the world as it has been reconciled to God has already appeared' (*CD* IV/3 314). The remaining paragraphs, §§ 71–3, headed 'The vocation of man', 'The Holy Spirit and the sending of the

Christian community', and 'The Holy Spirit and Christian hope', expand on this theme in suggestive, inventive and creative ways.

The Christian life

Despite an obvious diminution of energy, Barth was still working on the *Church Dogmatics* in his eighties, though he realized it would never reach completion. *CD* IV/4 had been planned as the ethics of reconciliation. He was keen to see at least one section published, and 'The foundation of the Christian life', a 'fragment' of *CD* IV/4, appeared in 1967. It was on the doctrine of baptism, and in it he took further the critique of the sacramental nature of the ordinance and the rite of infant baptism that he had first expounded in his controversial lecture of 1943 (see Chapter 7). The fact that he envisaged baptism as an aspect of ethics was striking enough. On its publication the fragment was wrongly interpreted as a contribution to sacramental theology, which it was never intended to be. Rather it is in keeping with Barth's concept of the recipient's free response to grace as the basis of the obedient life. Baptism, being the beginning of the Christian life, is continued in Eucharistic thankfulness, for which the Lord's Supper would be the symbol (on this, alas, Barth did not live to write). In other words, both baptism and the Eucharist belong to the ethical realm and are not, as such, 'means of grace'. Christ himself is the only sacrament, and Christ's baptism was in the Spirit. The thrust of Barth's ethical understanding of the sacraments became clearer in 1975 with the posthumous publication of § 74 and §§ 76–8, under the title of *The Christian Life*, 'Barth's last great piece of writing'.[4]

The groundwork of the ethics of reconciliation is laid out in § 74. In common with the ethical sections of each of the preceding volumes, God commands obedience, but in a participatory and creative rather than coercive way. The key concept is that of 'invocation', and the narrative context is the Lord's Prayer.

By invoking God, the human creature lives freely and confidently as a child of the heavenly Father: 'The humble and resolute ... invocation of the gracious God in gratitude, praise and ... petition [is] ... the normal action corresponding to the fulfilment of the covenant in Jesus Christ' (*CL* 43). Baptism, as the rite of initiation, can only be understood in terms of the human obedience that corresponds to God's redemptive work in Christ. It is 'a human activity corresponding to the divine activity' (*CD* IV/4 19). In §§ 76–8, 'The children and their Father', 'Zeal for the honour of God' (which contains the superb sub-section entitled 'The great passion'), and 'The struggle for human righteousness', is constituted a moving if unfinished treatment of the opening petitions of the Lord's Prayer in which the now familiar notes are struck: it is God himself through the Spirit who imparts the ability for men and women, already covenant partners through their gracious election in Christ, to fulfil their obligations and respond to his will: 'He is their free Father, not in a lofty isolation in which he would be the prisoner of his own majesty, but in his history with them as his free children whom he himself has freed' (*CL* 103). With the coming of the kingdom, invoked in prayer and echoed in an active obedience by those who pray, 'the lordless powers' are challenged ultimately to be vanquished by the victorious Christ. Although only God himself will inaugurate the kingdom, free human action is legitimized and taken up into the dynamic of God's unique action in Christ. With these striking paragraphs, Barth's lifelong project came to an end.

Karl Barth died, aged 82, on 10 December 1968. Although in poor health, his final two years had been productive, cheerful and fulfilled. He still led a seminar group and kept up an animated correspondence, mostly with Protestant pastors, Catholic theologians, many lay people and interested inquirers. He knew, however, that he was out of favour with the religious establishment, still enamoured as it was with secular theology. Following a period of neglect during the 1970s and 1980s there came a wave of renewed appreciation for his work, especially following the centenary year of 1986, and since then Barth's contribution has been studied with unprecedented acumen, diligence and perceptiveness. His stature as the one theologian of genius granted to the Church in our time is secure:

> In the midst of this ongoing engagement with his thought, Barth has come to be considered by many not simply as the outstanding voice of the twentieth century, but also as one of the most significant theologians in the history of the Christian church.[5]

The final word, however, should be allowed to Karl Barth himself:

> The last word I have to say . . . is not a concept like grace but a name: Jesus Christ. He is grace and he is the ultimate One beyond world and Church and even beyond theology. We cannot lay hold of him. But we have to do with him. And my own concern in my long life has been increasingly to emphasize this name and to say, 'In him'. There is no salvation but in this name. In him is grace. In him is the spur to work, warfare and fellowship. In him is all that I have attempted in my life in weakness and folly. It is there in him.   (*FT* 29–30)

Notes

1 Young man Barth

1 From the unpublished Geneva sermons, quoted in Eberhard Busch, *Barth*, Abingdon Pillars of Theology (Nashville: Abingdon Press, 2008), p. 2.

2 The pastor of Safenwil

1 B. Jaspert (ed.), *Karl Barth–Rudolf Bultmann, Letters 1922–66* (Edinburgh: T. & T. Clark, 1982), p. 154.

2 Jaspert (ed.), *Karl Barth–Rudolf Bultmann, Letters*, p. 153.

3 James D. Smart (ed.), *Revolutionary Theology in the Making: Barth–Thurneysen Correspondence, 1914–25* (London: Epworth Press, 1964), p. 22.

4 Quoted in Eberhard Busch, *Karl Barth: His Life from Letters and Autobiographical Texts* (London: SCM Press, 1976), p. 90.

5 Smart (ed.), *Revolutionary Theology in the Making*, p. 26.

6 Smart (ed.), *Revolutionary Theology in the Making*, p. 43.

7 Jaspert (ed.), *Karl Barth–Rudolf Bultmann, Letters*, p. 155.

8 Jaspert (ed.), *Karl Barth–Rudolf Bultmann, Letters*, p. 155.

9 Quoted in John McConnachie, *The Significance of Karl Barth* (London: Hodder & Stoughton, 1931), p. 37.

10 Smart (ed.), *Revolutionary Theology in the Making*, p. 59.

3 Göttingen and Münster

1 B. Jaspert (ed.), *Karl Barth–Rudolf Bultmann, Letters 1922–66* (Edinburgh: T. & T. Clark, 1982), p. 156.

2 James D. Smart (ed.), *Revolutionary Theology in the Making: Barth–Thurneysen Correspondence, 1914–25* (London: Epworth Press, 1964), p. 81.

3 Smart (ed.), *Revolutionary Theology in the Making*, p. 101.

4 Smart (ed.), *Revolutionary Theology in the Making*, p. 115.

5 The translations from *DE* offered here and later in this chapter are my own.

6 Adolf von Harnack, 'Open letter to Professor Karl Barth', in H. Martin Rumscheidt, *Revelation and Theology: An Analysis of the Barth–Harnack Correspondence of 1923* (Cambridge: Cambridge University Press, 1975), pp. 35–9 [39].

7 Karl Barth, 'An answer to Professor Adolf von Harnack's open letter', in Rumscheidt, *Revelation and Theology*, pp. 40–52 [49].

8 Karl Barth, 'Foreword', in Heinrich Heppe, *Reformed Dogmatics* (London: Allen & Unwin, 1950), pp. v–vii [v].

9 Smart (ed.), *Revolutionary Theology in the Making*, p. 176.

10 Smart (ed.), *Revolutionary Theology in the Making*, p. 185.

11 Smart (ed.), *Revolutionary Theology in the Making*, p. 221.

12 Barth, 'Foreword', Heppe, *Reformed Dogmatics*, p. v.

13 See Renate Köbler, *In the Shadow of Karl Barth: Charlotte von Kirschbaum* (Louisville, KY: Westminster John Knox Press, 1989), in which the matter is treated with sympathy and sensitivity, and the far more critical account by Suzanne Selinger, *Charlotte von Kirschbaum and Karl Barth: A Study in Biography and the History of Theology* (University Park, PA: University of Pennsylvania Press, 1998).

14 Rose Marie Barth, 'Prologue', in Köbler, *In the Shadow of Karl Barth*, p. 16.

4 The Bonn years

1 Quoted in Eberhard Busch, *Karl Barth: His life from Letters and Autobiographical Texts* (London: SCM Press, 1976), p. 190.

2 John McConnachie, *The Significance of Karl Barth* (London: Hodder & Stoughton, 1931), p. 60.

3 B. Jaspert (ed.), *Karl Barth–Rudolf Bultmann, Letters 1922–66* (Edinburgh: T. & T. Clark, 1982), p. 49.

4 T. H. L. Parker, *Karl Barth* (Grand Rapids: Eerdmans, 1970), p. 96.

5 John Baillie (ed.), *Natural Theology: Comprising 'Nature and Grace' by Emil Brunner, and 'No!' by Karl Barth* (London: Geoffrey Bles, 1946), p. 35.

6 Brunner, in Baillie (ed.), *Natural Theology*, p. 59.

7 Barth, in Baillie (ed.), *Natural Theology*, p. 121.
8 Barth, in Baillie (ed.), *Natural Theology*, p. 121.
9 Ivor Oswy Davies, 'Karl Barth', *Y Drysorfa* 112 (1942), pp. 44–9 [46]; the present translation from the Welsh is mine.
10 Quoted in Eberhard Busch, *Karl Barth: His Life from Letters and Autobiographical Texts* (London: SCM Press, 1976), p. 290.

5 The doctrine of the Word of God

1 John Webster, *Barth: Outstanding Christian Thinkers* (London: Continuum, 2000), p. 57.
2 George Hunsinger, *How to Read Karl Barth: The Shape of his Theology* (Oxford: Oxford University Press, 1991), p. 32.
3 Webster, *Barth*, p. 62.

6 The doctrine of God

1 Colin E. Gunton, *Act and Being: Towards a Theology of the Divine Attributes* (London: SCM Press, 2002), p. 9.
2 Bruce L. McCormack, 'Grace and Being', in John Webster (ed.), *The Cambridge Companion to Karl Barth* (Cambridge: Cambridge University Press, 2000), pp. 92–110 [92].
3 Karl Barth, 'Foreword', in Pierre Maury, *Predestination and Other Papers* (London: SCM Press, 1960), pp. 15–18 [16].
4 Colin E. Gunton, *The Barth Lectures* (London: T. & T. Clark, 2007), p. 121.

7 The doctrine of creation

1 E. Gordon Rupp, *'I Seek my Brethren': Bishop George Bell and the German Churches* (London: Epworth Press, 1974), p. 27.
2 Stanley Hauerwas, *With the Grain of the Universe: The Church's Witness and Natural Theology* (London: SCM Press, 2002), p. 179.
3 George S. Hendry, *Theology of Nature* (Philadelphia: Westminster Press, 1981), p. 25.
4 G. C. Berkouwer, *The Triumph of Grace in the Theology of Karl Barth* (Grand Rapids: Eerdmans, 1956), p. 23.
5 Joseph L. Mangina, *Karl Barth: Theologian of Christian Witness* (Aldershot: Ashgate, 2004), p. 87.

6 George Hunsinger, *How to Read Karl Barth: The Shape of his Theology* (Oxford: Oxford University Press, 1991), p. 34.

7 W. A. Whitehouse, *The Authority of Grace: Essays in Response to Karl Barth* (Edinburgh: T. & T. Clark, 1981), p. 51.

8 Mangina, *Karl Barth*, p. 143.

8 The doctrine of reconciliation

1 John Webster, *Barth: Outstanding Christian Thinkers* (London: Continuum, 2000), p. 113.

2 T. F. Torrance, *Karl Barth: Biblical and Evangelical Theologian* (Edinburgh: T. & T. Clark, 1990), p. 133.

3 For Korah see the Old Testament book of Numbers, ch. 16.

4 Webster, *Barth*, p. 156.

5 John R. Franke, *Barth for Armchair Theologians* (Louisville, KY: Westminster John Knox Press, 2006), pp. ix–x.

A guide to further reading

Church Dogmatics

Barth's major work, *Die kirchliche Dogmatik* (1932–67), has been translated as *Church Dogmatics*, edited by T. F. Torrance and Geoffrey W. Bromiley and published between 1956 and 1975 in 14 volumes, including an index volume, by T. & T. Clark. This is the edition used and referenced in the writing of this book. A new study edition of the whole of *Church Dogmatics* was issued in 2009, utilizing the earlier edition and keeping to the same plan but with adaptations geared to a modern theological studentship, and redistributed across 31 paperback volumes (and also available digitally; see <www.continuumbooks.com> for further details).

Table 2 provides a breakdown of the 14-volume edition of *Church Dogmatics*:

Table 2 The 14-volume edition of *Church Dogmatics*

Vol.	Subtitle and Barth's part/vol. number	Paragraphs	Chapters
1	*The Doctrine of the Word of God* I/1	§§ 1–12	Intro., 1, 2(i)
2	*The Doctrine of the Word of God* I/2	§§ 13–24	2(ii, iii), 3, 4
3	*The Doctrine of God* II/1	§§ 25–31	5, 6
4	*The Doctrine of God* II/2	§§ 32–9	7, 8
5	*The Doctrine of Creation* III/1	§§ 40–2	9
6	*The Doctrine of Creation* III/2	§§ 43–7	10
7	*The Doctrine of Creation* III/3	§§ 48–51	11
8	*The Doctrine of Creation* III/4	§§ 52–6	12
9	*The Doctrine of Reconciliation* IV/1	§§ 57–63	13, 14
10	*The Doctrine of Reconciliation* IV/2	§§ 64–8	15
11	*The Doctrine of Reconciliation* IV/3i	§§ 69–70	16
12	*The Doctrine of Reconciliation* IV/3ii	§§ 71–3	16 (cont.)
13	*The Doctrine of Reconciliation* IV/4	Fragment	
14	*Index*, with aids for the preacher		

G. T. Thomson's 1936 translation of *CD* I/1 under the title *The Doctrine of the Word of God* was superseded by Geoffrey W. Bromiley's 1975 version, which is uniform with the rest of the 14-volume series. A fragment of *CD* IV/4 was published as *The Christian Life* in 1981 (Edinburgh: T. & T. Clark).

Other works by Barth

Against the Stream: Shorter Post-War Writings, 1946–52 (London: SCM Press, 1954), trans. with intro. Ronald Gregor Smith.

Anselm: Fides Quaerens Intellectum (London: SCM Press, 1960), trans. Ian W. Robertson.

Die christliche Dogmatik im Entwurf (Munich: Christian Kaiser Verlag, 1927). (Note: no English edition exists; quotes provided in this book are the author's own translations.)

Come, Holy Spirit, a volume of sermons authored jointly with Eduard Thurneysen (London: Hodder & Stoughton, 1934; new edition Grand Rapids: Eerdmans, 1978), trans. Elmer Homrighausen and George W. Richards.

Deliverance to the Captives (London: SCM Press, 1961), trans. Marguerite Weiser.

Dogmatics in Outline (London: SCM Press, 1949; new edition, with foreword by Colin Gunton, London: SCM Press, 2001), trans. G. T. Thomson.

The Epistle to the Romans (Oxford: Oxford University Press, 1933; paperback edition 1968), trans. Edwyn C. Hoskyns.

Evangelical Theology: An Introduction (London: Collins, 1963), trans. Grover Foley.

Final Testimonies (Grand Rapids: Eerdmans, 1977), trans. Geoffrey W. Bromiley.

Fragments Grave and Gay (London: Collins, 1971), trans. Eric Mosbacher.

The Holy Ghost and the Christian Life (London: F. Muller, 1939; new edition entitled *The Holy Spirit and the Christian Life*, with foreword by Robin Lovin, Louisville, KY: Westminster John Knox Press, 1993), trans. R. Birch Hoyle.

How I Changed My Mind, intro. and epilogue John D. Godsey (Richmond, VA: John Knox Press, 1966).

The Humanity of God (London: Collins, 1961), trans. J. N. Thomas and Thomas Weiser.

Karl Barth's Table Talk, ed. John D. Godsey (Edinburgh: Oliver & Boyd, 1963).

The Knowledge of God and the Service of God (London: Hodder & Stoughton, 1938; new edition Eugene, OR: Wipf & Stock, 2005), trans. J. L. M. Hare and Ian Henderson.

A Letter to Great Britain from Switzerland (London: Sheldon, 1941; new edition Eugene, OR: Wipf & Stock, 2004).

Letters, 1961–68 (Edinburgh: T. & T. Clark, 1981), trans. Geoffrey W. Bromiley.

The Resurrection of the Dead (London: Hodder & Stoughton, 1933; new edition Eugene, OR: Wipf & Stock, 2003), trans. H. J. Stenning.

The Teaching of the Church Regarding Baptism (London: SCM Press, 1948; new edition Eugene, OR: Wipf & Stock, 2006), trans. Ernest A. Payne.

Theological Existence Today! (London: Hodder & Stoughton, 1933), trans. R. Birch Hoyle.

Theology and Church: Shorter Writings 1920–28 (London: SCM Press, 1962), trans. Louise P. Smith.

The Word of God and the Word of Man (London: Hodder & Stoughton, 1928; second edition with new foreword, San Francisco: Harper & Row, 1957), trans. Douglas Horton.

Posthumously published lecture series

Ethics (1928–9) (Edinburgh: T. & T. Clark, 1981), trans. Geoffrey W. Bromiley.

The Göttingen Dogmatics: Instruction in the Christian Religion, Vol. 1 (1924–5) (Grand Rapids: Eerdmans, 1991), trans. Geoffrey W. Bromiley. (Note: no English translation of volume 2 has in fact been published.)

The Theology of John Calvin (1922) (Grand Rapids: Eerdmans, 1995), trans. Geoffrey W. Bromiley.

The Theology of the Reformed Confessions (1923) (Louisville, KY: Westminster John Knox Press, 2002), trans. Darrell and Judith Guder.

The Theology of Schleiermacher (1923–4) (Edinburgh: T. & T. Clark, 1982), trans. Geoffrey W. Bromiley.

Works on Barth

The amount of scholarship on Barth is phenomenal. The books below and those listed in the endnotes to each chapter are only a small selection of what is available.

Hans Urs von Balthasar, *The Theology of Karl Barth: Exposition and Interpretation* (San Francisco: Ignatius, 1992).

Nigel Biggar (ed.), *Reckoning with Barth* (Oxford: Mowbrays, 1986).

Nigel Biggar, *The Hastening that Waits: Karl Barth's Ethics* (Cambridge: Cambridge University Press, 1993).

Eberhard Busch, *Karl Barth: His Life from Letters and Autobiographical Texts* (second edition, London: SCM Press, 1994).

Eberhard Busch, *The Great Passion: An Introduction to Karl Barth's Theology* (Grand Rapids: Eerdmans, 2004).

Eberhard Busch, *Barth*, Abingdon Pillars of Theology (Nashville, TN: Abingdon, 2008).

John R. Franke, *Barth for Armchair Theologians* (Louisville, KY: Westminster John Knox Press, 2006).

Timothy Gorringe, *Karl Barth: Against Hegemony* (Oxford: Oxford University Press, 1999).

Colin E. Gunton, *Becoming and Being: The Doctrine of God in Barth and Hartshorne* (second edition, London: SCM Press, 2002).

Colin E. Gunton, *The Barth Lectures* (London: T. & T. Clark, 2007).

Trevor Hart, *Regarding Karl Barth* (Carlisle: Paternoster, 1999).

Stanley Hauerwas, *With the Grain of the Universe: The Church's Witness and Natural Theology* (London: SCM Press, 2002).

George Hunsinger, *How to Read Karl Barth: The Shape of his Theology* (New York: Oxford University Press, 1991).

George Hunsinger, *Disruptive Grace: Studies in the Theology of Karl Barth* (Grand Rapids: Eerdmans, 2000).

Bruce L. McCormack, *Karl Barth's Critically Realistic Dialectical Theology* (Oxford: Oxford University Press, 1995).

Joseph L. Mangina, *Karl Barth: Theologian of Christian Witness* (Aldershot: Ashgate, 2004).

T. F. Torrance, *Karl Barth: Biblical and Evangelical Theologian* (Edinburgh: T. & T. Clark, 1990).

John Webster, *Karl Barth's Ethics of Reconciliation* (Cambridge: Cambridge University Press, 1995).

John Webster, *Barth's Moral Theology* (Edinburgh: T. & T. Clark, 1998).

John Webster, *Barth: Outstanding Christian Thinkers* (London: Continuum, 2000).

John Webster (ed.), *The Cambridge Companion to Karl Barth* (Cambridge: Cambridge University Press, 2000).

Index

Index